SYSTEMIC SOCIOLOGY

SYSTEMIC SOCIOLOGY

RAMKRISHNA MUKHERJEE

SAGE Publications
New Delhi ■ Thousand Oaks ■ London

First published in 1993 by

Sage Publications India Pvt Ltd.
M–32 Greater Kailash Market, I
New Delhi 110 048

Sage Publications Inc
2455 Teller Road
Thousand Oaks, California 91320

Sage Publications Ltd
6 Bonhill Street
London EC2A 4PU

Published by Tejeshwar Singh for Sage Publications India Pvt Ltd, photo-typeset by Vijaya Enterprises and printed at Chaman Enterprises.

Library of Congress Cataloging–in–Publication Data

Mukherjee, Ramkrishna.
   Systemic sociology/Ramkrishna Mukherjee.
      p.   cm.
   1. Sociology.   I. Title.
   HM51. M77 301—dc20 · 1993   93–5205
ISBN: 81–7036–352–7 (India-HB)   0–8039–9126–6 (US-HB)
      81–7036–353–5 (India-PB)   0–8039–9127–4 (US-PB)

In memory of
I.P. Desai

CONTENTS

INTRODUCTORY

I

Sociology denotes the science of society, but there is also a distinctive body of knowledge called social science. It is necessary, therefore, to specify the role of sociology under the aegis of social science. Such an effort will be inadequate if we merely state that sociology is a scientific discipline—like, for instance, economics, political science, and psychology—all belonging to the realm of social science. Moreover, this kind of a *systematic* arrangement alone of social science *specializations* will be false because the disciplines (in fact, the specializations) will not be geared to a unity. Therefore, it is necessary to examine how sociology as a specialization (like economics, etc.) forms a mutually exclusive part of a complex whole, namely, the social sciences as a system. This may be noted as the subject matter of *systemic* sociology.

Viewed in this manner, systemic sociology is concerned with (*i*) the nature of being a society, i.e., its ultimate substance, and (*ii*) the nature, sources and limits of knowledge with regard to society. The first component deals with the ontology of sociology for the sake of understanding society. The second deals with the epistemology of sociology in the perspective of the grounds of knowledge concerning all specializations in social science, including sociology as one of them. Then, the appraisal (and not merely the understanding) of society depends upon a systematic treatment of these two components of systemic sociology.

However, both the components of systemic sociology are concerned with abstractions. An analytic discussion of the subject matter may therefore be difficult to follow without preparing one's mind for it. This is so because our immediate perception of reality is synoptic and not analytic. It affords a general survey of affairs which may later be appraised analytically. We may, therefore, pose as illustration two facets of social reality which will facilitate our entry into discussions on the ontology and epistemology of sociology, respectively.

One of the chosen illustrations is the Indian joint family: its persistence and disintegration. This will facilitate our understanding of the substance of society. The emergence of Bangladesh in the subcontinent of India is the second illustration, which deals with the grounds of knowledge on society.

II

In the second half of the present century our spontaneous perception of reality is that the Indian joint family is breaking down. The joint family in India is in most cases patrilineal and patrivirilocal (i.e., the males live in the families of their fathers and the females move into the families of their husbands after marriage). In a classically conceived joint family, which may not have been uncommon in India in the nineteenth century, there is the patriarch *(karta)*, his wife, sons, their wives, sons' sons and their wives and unmarried children, and unmarried daughters and granddaughters from the male side (if any).

Rarely was (and is) a joint family of more than four generations, as portrayed above, because in most cases the patriarch's and his wife's span of life would not allow it. Such a family is schematically shown in Figure 1.

However, viewed from the most ancient generation (G4 in Figure 1), the Indian joint family need not only be the unilaterally joint family of procreation of a man and his wife. The man and his wife at G4 of Figure 1 will eventually pass away, but the joint family may be maintained by their sons living together, with their progeny. The family would now be characterized as the joint family of orientation of the male members ('brothers') located at the topmost generation level G3, as shown schematically in Figure 2.

The joint family will persist even though the 'brothers' in G3 of Figure 2 may separately form unilateral joint families of procreation of their sons, sons' wives, and their progeny. The joint family will still be maintained if a 'son'

FIGURE 1
Unilateral Joint Family of Procreation of Four Generations
(G1-G4)

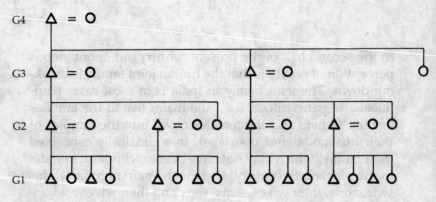

Δ: Male;   O: Female;   =: Marriage

FIGURE 2
Collateral Joint Family of Orientation of Three Generations
(G1-G3)

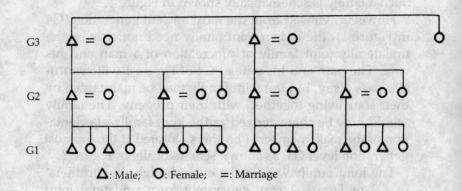

Δ: Male;   O: Female;   =: Marriage

FIGURE 3
Unilateral Joint Families of Procreation of Two Separated Brothers at the Third Generation

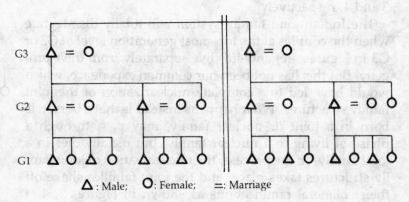

△ : Male;　○: Female;　=: Marriage

FIGURE 4
Unilateral Joint Families of Procreation of Three or Two Generations and Formation of Nuclear Families

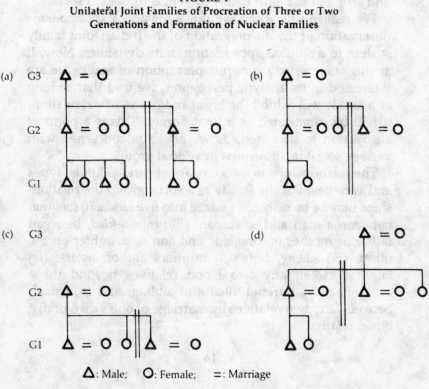

△: Male;　○: Female;　=: Marriage

15

of the separated 'brothers' in G3 of Figure 2 sets up a nuclear family with his wife and with or without children. These two possibilities are schematically depicted in Figures 3 and 4, respectively.

The Indian joint family system will totally disintegrate when the couples at the top-most generation level of G2 or G3 in Figures 4(c) and 4(d) live separately from their progeny. But this has not been our common experience, which would have led to a complete nuclearization of the joint family structures. What happens instead is that a person is born in a joint or nuclear family, may pass through a phase of living in a nuclear family, but usually dies in a joint family. In the process, the nuclearization of joint family structures takes place, and the joint families shake off their collateral ramifications as shown in Figures 3, 4(a) and 4(b); but the joint family system is upheld in society.

We realize this when we move beyond a spontaneous observation of the disintegration of the Indian joint family system to a studied appreciation of its dynamics. Now, if at this stage of still synoptic perception of reality we are interested in its analytic perception, we find that so long as a family will exhibit the lineal and/or the affinal relation, it will be constituted as a joint family. This is a point of abstraction to be noted, as we are thus concerned with various social relationships in a social group.

The relationships in a society are of various kinds, types and varieties. For the family as a social group the relationships may be broadly categorized into five kinds: (*i*) *conjugal*, between a man and a woman; (*ii*) *parental-filial*, between father or mother on one side and son or daughter on the other; (*iii*) *sibling*, between brothers and/or sisters; (*iv*) *lineal*, between any two blood relatives beyond those categorized as parental-filial and sibling; and (*v*) *affinal*, between any two relatives by marriage of one's own or of a blood relative.

Two points should be noted in the present context. First, when, in a nuclear family, a son brings in his wife, it is transformed into a joint family with the affinal relation between the parents-in-law and the daughter-in-law. The lineal relation may follow with the son's wife begetting a child. Conversely, with the absence of lineal and affinal relations within it, a nuclear family is formed when a 'son' separates from his parental family along with his wife and unmarried children (if any).

Second, while a lineal and/or affinal relation is the definitive criterion of existence of the joint family, for the patrilineal, partrivirilocal family, these relations are only of a few kinds out of all that is possible within the kinship system. They refer to the paternal male side of the family, the males, consorts and children. However, they are of different types because of generational distance between two family members, and may be of many varieties because of the collateral expansion of the family.

Thus, a lineal relation may be categorized as that between cousins and only from the paternal side in an Indian joint family. However, it may be of such varieties as father's brother's son or unmarried daughter, father's father's brother's son's son or unmarried daughter, as seen in Figures 1 and 2. All these details are presented in Table 1.

The analytic perception of reality, condensed in Figures 1 to 4 and Table 1, elicits the fact that, contrary to common belief, the mother-in-law versus daughter-in-law rivalry is not the main reason for the disintegration of the Indian joint family system. It remains endemic to the system, and may cause perennial tension in the family. However, not only in the context of its flourishing condition (as shown in Figures 1 to 3) but in its most attenuated form as well (Figure 4), the mother-in-law in her old age stays with one (or more) daughter-in-law.

The crux of the matter is then: Why do the sons separate

Table 1

Social Relationships in Indian Joint Family Structures as shown in Figures 1 to 4

Generational Distance	Collateral Distance	Social Relationship			Refers to Figures 1 2, 3, 4
		Kind	Type	Varieties	
None (as within G1, G2, G3 or G4)	None	Conjugal	–	H, W	1–4
	1	Sibling	–	B, Su	1–4
		Affinal	Sibling-in-law	BW, HSu	1–3
	2	Lineal	Cousin Order 1	FBZ, FBDu	1–3
		Affinal	"	FBZW	1–3
	3	Lineal	Cousin Order 2	FFBZZu, FFBZDu	1–2
One (as between G1 & G2, G2 & G3, G3 & G4)	None	Parental-filial	–	F, M	1–4
	1	Affinal	Parent-in-law	HF–ZW, HM–ZW	1–4
		Lineal	Avuncular: Order 1	FB–BZ/BDu, FSu–BZ/BDu	1–3, 4(a), 4(b)

(Table 1 Contd.)

Generational Distance	Collateral Distance	Social Relationship		Varieties	Refers to Figures 1 2, 3, 4
		Kind	Type		
	2	Affinal	Avuncular: Order 1	FBW–HBZ/HBDu	1–3, 4(a), 4(b)
		Lineal	Avuncular: Order 2	FFBZ–FBZZ, FFBDu–FBZDu	1–2
		Affinal	"	FFBZW–HFBZZ FFBZW–HFBZDu	1–2
Two (as between G1 & G3, G2 & G4)	None	Lineal	Grand-parental	FF–ZZ/ZDu FM–ZZ/ZDu	1–3, 4(a), 4(b)
		Affinal	Grandparent-in-law	HFF–ZZW HFM–ZZW	1
	1	Lineal	Grand Avuncular	FFB–BZZ/BZDu FFSu–BZZ/BZDu	1–2
		Affinal	"	FFBW–HBZZ/ HBZDu	1–2
Three (as between G1 & G4)	None	Lineal	Great-grand-parental	FFF–ZZZ/ZZDu FFM–ZZZ/ZZDu	1

F: father; M: mother; B: brother; S: sister; Z: son; D: daughter; H: husband; W: wife; u: unmarried.

from the paternal family and form nuclear family structures? Is it because of sibling rivalry or, more appropriately, because of the fomentation of sibling-in-law rivalry? If that be so, at what stage does the latter form of rivalry (in particular) emerge in the most acute form and cause a split in the joint family structure? Is it when the siblings have children or just after they are married?

Such hypotheses can now be formed for testing in empirical situations, from an analytic appreciation of the joint family structures. More hypotheses may be formed with regard to the shrinkage in the collateral expansion of the joint structures depicted in Figures 1 to 3. For instance, with reference to Figures 2 and 3, does the collateral joint family or 'brothers' break up because of sibling rivalry at G3, unequal emphasis on the parental vis-à-vis avuncular relationship between G3 and G2, inter-cousin relationships of near or distant order at G2, avuncular relationship of near or distant order between G1 and G2, and so on?

The formulation of these and similar hypotheses implies that a social relationship may be classified as one, but the social behaviour it anticipates and the sustained interactions between dyadic persons (the social actions) it observes vary by the order of distance within the classified relationship. For example, with reference to Table 1, we find that while with respect to a person or Ego, an FB (father's brother) and an FFBZ (father's father's brother's son) are both 'uncles', the manner in which the person behaves with these two uncles and actually interacts with them may not be the same. Similarly, the wives of two male siblings are expected to behave and interact like amiable sisters, but they might not.

Thus, from a synoptic to an analytic perception of reality regarding a social group like the Indian joint family, one may forsake some fallacious notions such as that concerning the mother-in-law and daughter-in-law rivalry assuming a crucial role in disintegrating the joint structures. At the same time, one may precisely steer the investigation toward an explanation of causality concerning the stability and change of the social group. In this context, a systemic relation between the concepts of social action, social behaviour, social relationship, and the institutional embodiment of the social group draws our primary attention in understanding society. This, therefore, will be discussed in Chapter 1 as one component of systemic sociology.

III

With the example of the Indian joint family we have so far been concerned with the ontology of sociology. If we now pay attention to the epistemology of sociology we find that while society is upheld and changes by means of diverse kinds of social groups, their institutions, relationships, behaviour and sustained actions, these manifestations are viewed from different aspects of society. One of these manifestations is labelled as cultural (= social), another as economic, still another as political or psychological, and so on. These variations have asserted their rights to autonomy and claim to be treated as distinctive social sciences. A confusion has thus emerged in the realm of knowledge because sociology is the science of society and not just a 'discipline' under what is now labelled social sciences.

This point rankled in the minds of pioneers in sociology and social science—Radha Kamal Mukerjee and D.P. Mukerji. D.P. explicitly stated in his 1955 Presidential Address to the First All India Sociological Conference:

Sociology has a floor and a ceiling, like any other science, but its speciality consists in its floor being the

21

ground-floor of all types of social disciplines, and its ceiling remaining open to the sky. In so far as they live on the same floor, they are bound to come into conflict with each other in the name of autonomy. But a stage comes when exclusiveness ceases to pay for the living (Mukerji 1958).

D.P.Mukerji thus points to the role of sociology in reference to social science, and notes the fissiparous tendencies in the realm of social science by adopting the label of social sciences. Both the points may be illustrated by examining the case of undivided Bengal, the partition of the subcontinent of India and the formation of the Eastern Wing of Pakistan—mainly comprising the territory of East Bengal—and the eventual emergence of Bangladesh from the Eastern Wing of Pakistan.

The growth of the Bengali ethnic unit presupposes at an early stage of social development, the identification of a territory as Bengal and the consolidation of its inhabitants to the extent that the mass of the people identified them - selves as *bāngālee*.* Long before 'Bengal' was used to denote a particular territory, the regions it integrated were known as *radh-desa, paundravardhana* and *gaur, samatata,* and *chattala*. West Bengal today comprises largely *radh-desa* and small portions of *gaura-paundravardhana* and *samatata*. The Eastern Wing of Pakistan (commonly known as East Pakistan) included the whole of *chattala* and the bulk of *gaura-paundravardhana* and *samatata*.

Little is known about the people in 'Bengal' before Aryanization began with the consolidation of the Gupta empire in eastern India from about the fifth century AD. It is known, however, that they were identified as *avira,*

---

* *'Bāngālee'* is the specific term used by the people to denote their ethnicity. 'Bengalee' and 'Bengali' became a generalized and anglicized identification.

bhilla, kamboga, khar, khas, kol, konch, mallo, pukkas, pundra, savara, sumba, etc. Those who lived in *samatata* and *chattala* (particularly in the forest areas) followed an arboreal economy and functioned within rather undifferentiated societies, as echoed in the ballads of *mymenshing gitika* and other forms of oral literature. Many other tribals (e.g., *koncha, mallo*) lived in the same or similar manner, while sufficient division of labour had taken place among some others (especially in *radh-desh*) to identify 'merchants' among food producers, food gatherers and handicraftsmen. The 'merchants' dealt mainly in betel leaf, areca nut, coconut, sugarcane and bee-honey.

However, these people lived more or less autonomously and in a rather undifferentiated state of social organization. Simple economy and rudimentary polity sustained their cultural identities while bringing them in contact with one another as and when the occasion arose. Therefore, the sociology of Bengal before the 'Bengalee' emerged on the scene required, on the one hand, a look at the base of a social frame—which is concerned with the substance of society in the forms of social action, behaviour, relationships, and institutions of the respective peoples for maintaining their identities. On the other hand, the sociology of Bengal required looking at the top of the social frame which expressed a conglomeration of these people by means of their alliance of culture, economy, polity, etc.

This dual role of sociology becomes clearer at later stages of Bengal's history, beginning with the emergence of a Bengali ethnicity. The social frame changed drastically in its form and content when the caste organization developed in Bengali society along with the importation of Brahmins by the rulers of Bengal from the west and south of India as religious and legal authorities. The indigenous people were labelled *sudra, antyaja, mlechcha,* and *yabana;* and, eventually, all people (including the Brahmins) were

23

categorized into respective *jatis* according to their vocations. The *jati* division of society became a hereditary
phenomenon which carried with it all the familiar caste
prohibitions against marriage, dining and physical contact
between people of different *jatis*. By the twelfth century
the caste organization had spread so much in extent and
depth that royal edicts placed the *jatis* in a hierarchical
order of 'purity'. Evidently, a Bengali ethnicity has emerged
in the territory known as Bengal.

However, the caste structure of Bengal did not have the
foundation or the stable growth found in the Indo-Gange-
tic plain proper. There was hardly any aspirant to the *varnas*
of Kshatriya (warrior) and Vaishya (husbandman). Only
later, and by which time the caste system was definitely
established in Bengal, did some of the rulers and wealthy
merchants ask for or usurp such recognition in society.
The attempt, however, was casual or transitory, as it is to
date. Thus, the sociology of the societies of Bengal and
Uttar Pradesh (say) had and have similarities and differences both in substance at the bottom of the social frame
and integration of the aspects of demography, culture,
economy, polity, etc., at the top of the same social frame.

Bengal society presented in these respects a specific
phenomenon in as much as that, pointedly, the Brahmani-
cal impositions on the society of Bengal were not a one-
way process. Because of the existence of powerful social
groups that were placed in ranks lower in the socio-religious
(= cultural) scale than that of the Brahmins, compromises
had to be made between the Brahmanic and the non-
Brahmanic ways of life. It is important to note in this context that the caste organization and the settlement of
people on land with plough cultivation went hand in hand
from about the fifth century AD, and by the twelfth and
thirteenth centuries both had become stabilized in Bengal
society. The indigenous peoples of Bengal accepted the

Brahmanic way of life because of the accompanying economic privileges of a settled agricultural society, but they also contributed significantly to the social organization and the ideology which eventually emerged in Bengal from this process of culture-contact.

As a result, while Hinduism spread over Bengal, the Bengali Hindus were particularly distinguished from their co-religionists in the rest of the subcontinent of India. Even today, orthodox Brahmins in other parts of India will not dine with Bengali Brahmins who eat fish and are also in other ways regarded to deviate from the vocation of the Brahmins. The Hindus of Bengal, thus, assumed a distinct 'Bengali' character. In order to appreciate this character precisely and comprehensively, the sociology of Hindu Bengal draws one's attention to its dual role at the base and the top of the social frame, as noted earlier.

While the Hindus of Bengal were thus ethnically consolidated and correspondingly alienated from the Hindus in the rest of India, the course of Hinduization was not the same in the eastern and the western regions of Bengal. The area east of the Padma river (a tributary of the Ganges), which comprised the bulk of East Bengal, was not easily accessible from the west. It was closely linked with Assam, where Buddhism and, later, a loose form of Hinduism prevailed. Buddhism contented itself with superimposing a new religion upon the existing tribal societies which it left largely unchanged with regard to the introduction of new economic activities and from which it did not even uproot animistic practices. Because of their remoteness from the seat of Hindu rule in *gaur*, the people of East Bengal were also relatively free from control by the Guptas and other Hindu rulers.

As a result of this symbiosis of culture, economy and polity, there developed a combination of creeds and cults, known as *sahajiya* ('simplified religion'), and the Brahmins from the western region of Bengal considered the area east of the Padma as defiling and detrimental to their status. Consequently, when in the wake of Muslim conquest the zeal of conversion to Islam was felt in Bengali society, the great majority of the people of East Bengal were converted. Some Muslims from the northern part of India no doubt settled in Bengal, and even some Brahmins were converted to Islam. But like the imported Brahmins among Bengali Hindus, they constituted a very small proportion of the Muslim population in both East and West Bengal.

Regional distinction thus coincided with religious differentiation, and both played their role in Bengali society. The forces of consolidation of 'Bengali' culture, economy and polity, however, were greater than these two forces of alienation. Muslim *sufism* (a branch of Islamic philosophy and religion) and Hindu *sahajiya* and Vaishnavism, as against orthodox religious systems, found a fertile soil in Bengal and helped in the development of a Bengali culture and a Bengali language. With the onset of the Bhakti movement in eastern India under Chaitanya's leadership, the Hindus and the Muslims were brought closer to each other on the social and ideological planes. The Hindus began to venerate the Muslim saints and, correspondingly, the Muslims paid homage to the Hindu saints. The Hindu god Satya Narayan became Satya Pir of the Muslims, the goddess Olai Chandi of the Hindus became Ola Bibi of the Muslims, and the Bauls of Bengal (nomads who sang the gospel of equality of all people irrespective of their religious faith and caste affiliation) were both Hindus and Muslims or, more accurately, a composite product of the two ideologies.

Also, from the time of Chaitanya (1485–1533), the Bengali language was raised to the status of a literary language and in course of time it was enriched with loan words and phrases from Persian and Arabic. The Muslim rulers actively supported these trends. The most important of all Hindu epics—the Ramayana, Mahabharata and Bhagavata—were translated from Sanskrit into Bengali under the patronage of Muslim rulers who also honoured both Hindu and Muslim noblemen and men of letters, and employed both Hindus and Muslims as state officials, revenue farmers (zamindars), etc.

The economic structure of Bengal at that time facilitated and consolidated the unity achieved in the social and ideological life of the people, for it involved Hindus and Muslims who followed the same or similar vocations in East and West Bengal. Just as there were Hindu priests and Muslim *mullahs* or Hindu and Muslim noblemen and zamindars, so were there Hindu and Muslim artisans, traders, peasants, etc. The *jati* or caste division of the people, which should not be confused with the *varna* or four-class distinction of the Hindus, had become so deep-rooted in society that many functional castes emerged among the Muslims. They maintained harmony in the social structure and held the society in balance. Cotton weaving had developed as an important industry in which were engaged the Hindu *tanti* and the Muslim *jolaha*. Fishing was an important occupation in riverine Bengal, in which were engaged the Hindu *jalia kaibarta*, *pods*, etc., and the Muslim *nikari*, *dhawa*, *mahifarash*, etc. The caste of oil-pressers included both the Hindu *kolu* and the Muslim *khulu*.

A Bengali ethnic unit had thus emerged irrespective of the regional and religious distinctions of the people, and it approached the point of attaining nationhood in the sixteenth to eighteenth centuries. The people of Bengal had a territorial identification, a common history, a community of culture and language, a common economic organization based on agriculture and industry (mainly the production of cotton and silk textiles demanded in the international market through the agencies of European East India Companies),

27

and a distinct psychological identity which was asserted against superior or analogous powers. Examples of the latter were the role of the *bar-bhuinyas*, the twelve feudatory lords of Bengal, who included both Hindus and Muslims and who sometimes combined, irrespective of religious faith, to overthrow the suzerainty of the Mughal rulers; the several attempts of the Nawabs of Bengal—who had both Hindu and Muslim generals and ministers—to declare the *subah* (province) of Bengal independent of the Mughal state power; and the sustained defence organized by the Bengalee against Maratha domination in the eighteenth century.

This course of nation-building of the Bengalee cannot be duly appreciated without an analysis of the regional and religious distinctions and similarities among the Bengalee, seen at both the previously explained base and the top of the social frame. And, that becomes particularly necessary when examining nation and state formations in Bengal under the British and contemporarily.

The economy and polity of Bengal suffered serious reverses in the first phase of British rule, which affected the Muslims more adversely than the Hindus. As it happened subsequently all over India, the disintegration of Bengal's industry and trade, and the devitalizaion of its agrarian economy, affected equally the Hindu and Muslim masses. But, from the time the English East India Company captured power in Bengal in 1757 and up to the middle of the nineteenth century when' India passed over to the British Crown, the Muslims were deliberately discriminated against in the field of administration and civic organization as well as in economic activities related to the interests of the Company and its officials. They were held in suspicion by the Company officials and were regarded as direct representatives of the previous rulers. The Muslim aristocrats also pursued a policy of aloofness from the

Company's activities. There were, of course, notable exceptions but, in general, they retreated to obscure stations or dispersed in the countryside, thereby losing the position of leadership in society which they had held previously along with their Hindu counterparts.

The Hindus, on the other hand, were favoured by the Company and its officials, although most of the previous Hindu revenue farmers, merchants, etc., were removed from the social scene. There were, however, other Hindus who closely aligned themselves with the Company and its officials, and as their agents (known as *baniyan* or *gomostha*), this group gained a strong footing in the economic organization of Bengal through dealings in its merchandise and other products. But, eventually, unlike their English counterparts, these persons were unable to thrive as merchants or to invest their gains in industrial production because the foreign ruler's policy was not conducive to such a course of development. They could, however, turn themselves into a landed aristocracy, especially after the Permanent Settlement of Land in Bengal from 1793.

In this pursuit East Bengal appeared to these landlords as a virgin field because 'Rajahs' were few and far between there. Consequently, by the middle of the nineteenth century the powerful landlords of East Bengal were Hindus, with a few exceptions like the Nawabs of Dacca, Bogra and Jalpaiguri. Moreover, subinfeudation followed in the wake of the Permanent Settlement of Land, and ever-increasing numbers of Hindus (who were in an advantageous position to accumulate some wealth) became subsidiary landlords. The process operated throughout Bengal, but in East Bengal it took the character of Hindu landlords versus Muslim peasantry since the latter constituted the bulk of the local population.

Because of their induced superiority in culture and

economy, the Hindus could usurp almost all the facilities then available for education, which even wealthy Muslims kept away from. As a result, the Bengali *baboos* (clerks) in the government and in the mercantile firms were virtually all Hindus. At the same time, while living on the rent from land, a dominant segment of the educated Hindus could employ their time in the pursuit of science, art and literature. Indeed, the social structure of Bengal had changed so much in about a century that the 1871 Census report of Bengal recorded:

> Hindus, with exception of course, are the principal *zemindars, talookdars* [owners of large subinfeudatory estates], public officers, men of learning, money-lenders, traders, shop-keepers, and [are] engaging in most active pursuits of life and coming directly and frequently under the notice of the rulers of the country; while the Musalmans, with exceptions also, form a very large majority of the cultivators of the ground and of the day labourers, and others engaged in the very humblest forms of mechanical skill and of buying and selling, as tailors, turban-makers, makers of huqqa-snakes, dyers, wood-polishers, oil sellers, sellers of vegetables and fish, and in few instances attracting the attention of those who do not mix much with the humbler classes of people, or make special inquiry into their occupations or circumstances (quoted in Khan 1960: 19).

The middle class that developed in Bengal by the end of the nineteenth century was thus composed almost entirely of Hindus, which affected the previously established harmony of Bengal's social structure and was felt more keenly in East Bengal because of its Muslim majority. Some Hindu intellectuals lamented the loss of Bengal because of the decay of Muslim literature and culture, but, in general, the Hindus remained oblivious to it. Moreover, their reaction to the situation was influenced by the resurgence, in the last quarter of the eighteenth century, of government supported religious orthodoxy in both communities, which tended to separate the Hindus and the Muslims who had previously been brought closer by the propagation of humanistic values.

In sum, because of the prevailing forces of economy and polity at the top of the society, the cultural base of interaction between the Hindus and the Muslims changed drastically. The upshot was that the dominant group of the Hindus began to show indifference and even contempt towards the Muslim way of life, and the latter group reacted sharply. In earlier times, the Muslims participated in the important Hindu festivals such as Durga Puja in autumn and Holi in spring, just as the Hindus participated in the Muslim festivals of Muharram and Id. But later these occasions frequently led to communal riots between Hindus and Muslims. A conflict situation which was perennial but not pervasive in earlier times, thus emerged and had a pernicious effect on the course of nation-building and state formation in Bengal.

Yet, the 'Bengali' identity remained. In 1905, there was such a powerful movement against the British proposal to divide Bengal administratively into east and west that the proposal had to be hastily withdrawn. It may be that the inter-community conflict, now in the open, failed to lead to a decisive rupture of Hindu–Muslim relations, although the anti-British stance displayed mostly by the Hindus from the second half of the nineteenth century had led the rulers to shift their support to the Muslim community: a support which the latter readily accepted in order to recover its social position and status. Muslim leaders persuaded the government to offer special facilities for education and job reservations for the Muslims and a Muslim middle class began to grow in Bengal, especially from the beginning of the twentieth century.

The concurrent shift in the agrarian economy of Bengal helped in the growth of the Muslim middle class. At the close of the nineteenth century, crops in Bengal were steadily acquiring a commodity value with the ever-growing external and home markets. Accordingly, although they formed a distinct minority in the total society, the peasants with substantial holdings which could not be cultivated solely by their own labour ceased to settle their surplus holdings on other peasants under the few contemporary tenures allowed under the rules of the Permanent Settlement of Land. Instead, they began to have these holdings cultivated by sharecroppers recruited from the ranks of impoverished peasants, since in this way they could acquire more land from the profitable concern and employ the newly acquired holdings for the same mode of production. Thus, a category known as *jotedar* (landholder) emerged in rural Bengal, distinct from the category of *zamindar* (landlord, and *not* revenue farmer) created by the Permanent Settlement of Land.

A distinct social group, displaying with others distinctive sets of social relationship, social behaviour and social action, came into operation because of changes in the economy with the commodification of crops. *Jotedars* were found in Bengal from way back in history, but, now, they emerged as a cohesive social group. Naturally, in the Muslim majority area of East Bengal an appreciable number of the *jotedars* were Muslims, and the number increased in course of time; some, like their Hindu counterparts, became petty zamindars in order to raise their social status.

Since most of the *jotedars* could afford the cost of higher education for their sons or provide them with capital to invest in business in neighbouring towns, a large number of *jotedar* families forged links with the urban middle class, as one or more of the family became a school or college teacher, a lawyer, doctor, businessman, government or civic official, clerk, etc. This process among both the Hindu and Muslim rural elites after 1920, and especially among the Muslims in the eastern region of Bengal, has been traced in intensive village and case studies. They show how the Muslim middle class could grow at a rapid rate after 1920 because Bengal, and particularly its eastern region, was overwhelmingly rural.

It thus appeared that the emergence of a new social structure in the first quarter of the present century would override regional and religious distinctions of the 'Bengali' people. It seemed likely that the propertied class of Hindus and Muslims would unite in relation to the impoverished but increasingly unified Hindu and Muslim peasantry and their like, and that further changes in Bengali society would be effected primarily on the economic plane, with repercussions in the social and ideological life of the people—their relationships, behaviour, and action on class lines. There were indications to support this prognosis. Leaders of the Muslim middle class, such as Moulvi A.K. Fazlul-Huq and Md. Azizul Huque, organized the Krishak Praja Party (literally, Peasants and Peoples Party) which remained restricted to Bengal and served essentially as the mouthpiece of *jotedar* interest in Bengal's economy and politics.

The party refrained from taking a religious or communal stand, and found members and allies among the Hindu middle class with substantial *jotedar* interest, as was evident from the Hindu members and supporters of local self-government formed by the party in Bengal. Both Moulvi Fazlul-Huq and Md. Azizul Huque had humble origins: the former becoming a lawyer, *jotedar*, and petty zamindar, and the latter, additionally, an educationist and at one time Vice-Chancellor of Calcutta University. Their party formed the provincial government of Bengal between 1937 and 1943. On the other hand, the peasant movement of Bengal, which flared up during the 1930s and the 1940s under the leadership of the Communist Party of India, was stronger in East Bengal and had a large following among both the Hindu and Muslim peasantry.

The Hindu middle class, however, was solidly entrenched in Bengal's economy and polity. The correspondingly Muslim interest could not compete with it even though it held political power from 1937. The urban population, the educated community, the landed interest and the bureaucracy of Bengal were still predominantly Hindu. Moreover, regionally, West Bengal (with its Hindu stronghold) held East Bengal (with its Muslim stronghold) as its hinterland.

In the circumstances, the Bengali Muslim middle class envisaged a quicker and easier way to further its interests by responding to the call of the All India Muslim League, which was steadily gaining strength with the demand of a Muslim homeland. In this way it expected to secure a territory and government of its own, as well as its own market in goods and services. Therefore, instead of pursuing only the Krishak Praja Party, Muslim leaders first aligned themselves with and later joined the Muslim League.

The Muslim bourgeoisie, now viable, began to manoeuvre the Muslim peasantry and growing working class (especially in East Bengal) through the influence they wielded in the countryside and with other variants of the Muslim elite. The Congress Party, with its core leadership representing the Hindu landed and business interests, was regarded by the Muslims as a Hindu organization. The Communist Party and other left-wing parties were not strong enough to check the communal drift. As a result, influenced by the supra-Bengal course of alienation in

India operating at the top of Bengal society, the religious-
and region-wise alienation of the 'Bengali' people won
over their ethnic and national identity. Nation-building
and state formation in Bengal took an unprecedented turn:
in 1947 the two regions of Bengal were awarded to two
newly created state formations—West Bengal to the Indian
Union and East Bengal to Pakistan. Thus, a drastic change
took place at the base of 'Bengali' society—in the social relationships, social behaviour, and social action of the
people.

It appeared that Bengali Muslim interests would have
free and full play in East Pakistan. The communal riots,
which preceded the partition of the subcontinent of India
and recurred in East Pakistan several times afterwards,
led to the migration of 3.14 million Bengali Hindus from
East Pakistan to West Bengal between 1947 and 1961. The
first to opt out were the government officials and big
businessmen who had substantial contacts with West Bengal, especially with Calcutta. The next were the professionals (e.g., doctors, lawyers, teachers), the rural elites
subsisting on petty zamindari or *jotedari* interests, and the
clerks in the government, commercial and industrial organi-
zations. The third drift was mainly of artisans, petty traders
and owner-cultivators. Those on the lowest rungs of the
economic ladder (viz., sharecroppers and agricultural
labourers) and only a sprinkling of Hindus otherwise
occupied (including some big businessmen, professionals
and rural elites) stayed in their homeland until the catas-
trophic happenings of 1971. The selective and successive
phases of migration of Hindus from East Pakistan facilitated the growth of a Muslim market in goods and services,
but Muslims indigenous to Bengal proved only partially
able to utilize the opportunities thus created.

In East Pakistan, the Bengali Muslims were permitted
rather easy access to the lower and middle ranges of

economic activities, especially to the professions of lawyer, teacher, doctor, etc.; but the top governmental, commercial and industrial positions virtually became the monopoly of West Pakistanis posted in East Bengal from the centre of gravity of Pakistan in Sind and West Punjab. Similarly, the big business interests, which flowered in East Bengal, were controlled by West Pakistanis or by Urdu-speaking refugee Muslims from central and northern India who had migrated to Bengal with capital and/or acumen and experience. As reported in an unpublished study conducted in the 1960s by an international research organization which must remain anonymous: 'Of the largest factories in the East Wing, including the largest, all but one are owned by non-Bengalis.' It was also found while analyzing the factors in Bengali regionalism in Pakistan that the manner in which the *paschimas* (people from West Pakistan) were supposed to be exploiting the East Bengalis was much the same as was formerly charged against the Hindus and the British.

Regional, linguistic and kinship ties strengthened the bonds between the East Pakistani top bureaucracy and big business, from which the Bengali Muslims were virtually barred. Moreover, law and order, together with security and defence of this wing of Pakistan, were almost entirely in the hands of West Pakistanis. The subservient position of the Bengali Muslims in the political and economic life of East Bengal was thus reinforced. The result was that the role of economy, governed by polity, affected the supposedly democratic way of life at the base of East Bengal society. A schism developed between East and West Pakistani Muslims, affecting the social relationship, behaviour, and action between the two Muslim communities.

In the first few years, however, the discriminatory situation was not apparent to the Bengali Muslims. Their middle class elements had not yet emerged sufficiently for them to aspire to the top positions in the governmental, commercial and industrial sectors. The Bengali Muslim elites, as well as the masses (with whom the former maintained live contact in rural and urban areas) were satisfied to fill the vacuum created by the emigration of Bengali Hindus from the middle stratum of economic activities, while the upper stratum was filled mainly by non-Bengali Muslims.

Nevertheless, although truncated at the top, the market in goods and services which the Bengali Muslims obtained with the advent of Pakistan facilitated the spread of education among their children. According to census figures, from 1951 to 1961, the percentage of literates to the total population (excluding readers of the Holy Quran) rose from 13 to 18. A sample survey of students in Dacca city in 1957 showed that 77 per cent of the university and undergraduate students came from villages; the mother-tongue of 93 per cent of them was Bengali, and for 50 per cent the father's education was under matriculation or none.

The Bengali Muslim middle class thus grew at a far more rapid rate than ever before, and within a few years the process began to provide an ever-increasing number of new aspirants for governmental, managerial and executive jobs, while the vacuum created by the displacement of the Hindu population from East Pakistan was soon overfilled. In addition, those who had previously occupied the middle rungs of the economic and political ladders began to chafe at the lack of opportunity to further improve their positions.

The upshot was that the Bengali Muslims' orientation to social change passed from the temporal· to the contemporary cross-cultural perspective of regional disparities. They were no longer concerned with their position before and after the establishment of Pakistan in East Bengal, but with contrasting the opportunities available in the Eastern and Western wings of the republic. A social process thus began to gather momentum among the Bengali Muslims to throw off the lid that was obstructing the course of development they had aspired to when they subscribed to the ideology of Pakistan in the last phase of British rule in India, namely, to possess a territory and government of their own and to control their own market in goods and services. With this new perspective they soon discovered that they were not only deprived of economic opportunities in their homeland, but that the fruits of their capital and labour were being utilized more for the betterment of West than East Pakistan.

The germ of the East Pakistanis' alienation from the West Pakistanis was present from the time the Bengali Muslims responded to the call of Pakistan. Mr. Jinnah, the architect of Pakistan, had declared that 'India is not a nation, nor a country' and that 'the Muslims are not a minority but a nation and self-determination is their birthright'. But when the Bengali Moulvi A.K. Fazlul-Huq moved the famous Lahore Resolution of 1940, in which the Muslim League demanded explicitly, for the first time, the creation of Pakistan, the wording of the Resolution made it clear that the demand was for two 'Pakistans', one of which would be in Bengal: 'The areas in which the Muslims are numerically in majority, as in the northwestern and eastern zones of India, should be grouped to constitute "independent states" in which the constituent units shall be autonomous and sovereign' (quoted in Callard 1957:158).

However, during the last few years of British rule the alienation of the Muslims from the Hindus overpowered the force of ethnic identity of the Bengalees. Correspondingly, the consolidation of the Muslims in the two wings of Pakistan was marked by the Bengalees in Pakistan identifying themselves primarily as Pakistanis. It thus appeared that the 'two-nation' theory of Mr. Jinnah was not merely a political manoeuvre: a nation was being built on the basis of the Muslim way of life.

Islamization of East Pakistan and Arabicization of the Bengali language and literature facilitated the course of religious consolidation. In addition to the fact that from 1948 on, frequent declarations of Pakistan as an Islamic state were no less enthusiastically received in the East than in the West Wing of Pakistan, the 1951 Census recorded 8.9 million people in East Pakistan as 'literates, including Holy Quran readers', of whom 3.3 million persons were exclusively of the latter category. A survey of under-graduate and postgraduate students in Dacca in 1957 showed that although Bengali was the mother-tongue for 93 per cent, 35 per cent of these Bengali students could read, write and speak Urdu, and 34 per cent could read and write Arabic; by contrast, only 2 per cent of those whose mother-tongue was not Bengali could read, write and speak Bengali.

Furthermore, the deliberate imposition of Arabic words upon the Bengali language and literature by the new enthusiasts was not resented at first. A possibility had thus opened up for the people of East Pakistan to drift farther away from those of West Bengal and forge a stronger link with those of West Pakistan, the *paschimas*. Seemingly, Bengali society was at the crossroads. The honeymoon, however, was soon over.

Economic and political discrimination against the East Pakistanis snapped the theocratic bond of all Pakistanis. Significantly, the 1961 Census recorded that the number of Holy Quran readers in East Pakistan had dropped from 3.3 million in 1951 to 1.7 million. Nation-building in East Pakistan again took a different turn.

In 1948 the grumblings of discontent were already being heard in the Constituent Assembly of Pakistan: 'A feeling is growing among the Eastern Pakistanis that Eastern

Pakistan is being neglected and treated merely as a "Colony" of Western Pakistan' (quoted in Sayeed 1967:64). Now, the consolidation as Bengalee began to re-emerge, corresponding to the alienation of the East from the West Pakistanis. It first took shape in the demand for Bengali as a national language, and climaxed in the police firing on demonstrators on 21 February 1952. The floodgate of a new nationalism in East Pakistan opened up, and this day has since been observed as the 'day of martyrs (Shahid Dibas)'.

In the new situation, the old leaders of the Bengali middle class became active again. Moulvi A.K. Fazlul-Huq, mover of the 1940 Lahore Resolution of the Muslim League, and his erstwhile colleagues such as Md. Azizul Huque, formed the Krishak Sramik Party (Peasants' and Workers' Party) in the image of their previously established Krishak Praja Party. This party, like its predecessor non-communal in character, demanded in its twelve point programme of 29 July 1953, recognition of Bengali as a state language and full regional autonomy for East Pakistan on the basis of the 1940 Lahore Resolution. However, the initiative passed from these older hands to such new leaders as Moulana Bhashani as well as Sheikh Mujibur Rahman who led the Awami League movement, launched a radical programme for the future of East Pakistan, and found the broadest response from the radical Muslim intellectuals, members of the national bourgeoisie, peasants, workers, and owners of small- and middle-sized landholdings.

In order to retain and consolidate its gains, the state retaliated with alternate measures of repression and concession, as had happened in the subcontinent of India during the last phase of British rule. And the results were also similar to those in British India: the adopted measures merely fed the ever-growing national upsurge of the East

Pakistanis, who categorically ceased to identify themselves as Pakistanis. Sheikh Mujibur Rahman, the leader of the people, became *Bangabandhu* (Friend of Bengal). On 17 April 1971, the territory of the Eastern Wing of Pakistan was renamed *Bangladesh* (The Land of Bengal). Afterwards, having passed through a phase of severe devastation, massacre and armed struggle against the Pakistan government, the free and sovereign state of Bangladesh was formed on 16 December 1971.

We have, thus, discussed at some length the formation of Bengali ethnicity and the emergence of Bangladesh for the purpose of demonstrating the fact that the sociology of any people is concerned, on the one hand, with the substance of the society at the base of the social frame and, on the other, with the integration of various manifestations of society (e.g., polity, economy and culture) at the top of the social frame. If we do not undertake the dual task, we may be swayed by unilateral explanations of the partition of the subcontinent of India and, later, the formation of Bangladesh.

For example, we may overemphasize the role of polity in accordance with the two-nation theory of Mr. Jinnah. We may assert the innate psychological tendency of Muslim separatism from the Hindus. Or, we may point to unequal exchange between the Western and the Eastern Wings of Pakistan in order to unilaterally vindicate the role of economy in the nation and state formation of Bangladesh. Alternatively, we may harp on culture—the ethnicity of being *bāngālee*—in the same context, without exploring the nuances of being *Bengali* Muslim or *Muslim* Bengali in the course of nation and state formation of Bangladesh.

Thus it is that sociology is concerned not only with the ontology of society but also its epistemology which requires integration of all social science specializations at the top of the social frame in view. However, the latter point deserves clarification in view of the manner in which the social science specializations are often treated by the social scientists. Therefore, this point, in particular, will be considered in Chapter 2.

IV

More examples than the foregoing may be cited to illustrate that it would not be possible to appreciate sociology systemically without examining its two terms of reference, viz., the ontology and epistemology of society. However, while that may not be necessary and the readers may not be tuned to an analytic perception of social reality, the point remains as to the purpose behind this kind of exercise in systemic sociology. Therefore, the *modus operandi* of perceiving social reality has been briefly discussed in this introductory volume as 'Concluding Remarks'. Following this, the reader may proceed toward a systematic appraisal of social reality, as demonstrated by the present writer in his two monographs entitled *The Quality of Life: Valuation in the Social Research* and *Society, Culture, Development*, both published by Sage, New Delhi, in 1989 and 1991, respectively.

1. UNDERSTANDING SOCIETY

A Variable Entity

An entity is a thing in existence, whatever may be its qualitative distinction and in whichever way it may be related to other entities. Correspondingly, society is a thing which has real existence but assumes various configurations. In this respect, there is no *directly identifiable* criterion by which society can be defined in only one and the same manner. We may formulate many criteria and find that society is characterized by one or a combination of them. However, none of them can be stipulated to be the criterion to define society. Also, a particular set of these criteria would be equally unfruitful. This is implied in the Concise Oxford Dictionary's meaning of 'society', which is the:

> Social mode of life, the customs and organization of a civilized nation, any social community, the upper classes of a community whose movements and entertainments and other doings are more or less conspicuous, the socially distinguished, fashionable and well-to-do and well-connected people, participation in hospitality, other people's houses or company, companionship, company, association of persons united by a common aim or interest.

We also find from our observations and experience that society is identified in various ways. The directly identifiable criteria of habitation of a common territory and exercise of a distinct political authority can distinguish societies. Indian society is thus distinguished from Bangladeshi or Pakistani society. But another directly identifiable criterion of language will concurrently distinguish Punjabi society by consolidating its components from Indian and Pakistani societies. Bengali society would be similarly constituted by consolidating Bangladeshi society with the West Bengal component of Indian society. On the other hand, Bengali and Punjabi societies may refer exclusively to the respective components of Indian society.

One may also consider that these criteria are superseded by the criterion of religion to denote Hindu society, Muslim society, etc. Alternatively, this criterion may be employed to denote Hindu Bengali society, Muslim Bengali society, Hindu Punjabi society, Muslim Punjabi society, etc. These societies may also be identified by employing, additionally, the previous two criteria of common territory and political authority and, thus, within the respective jurisdictions of Indian, Bangladeshi and Pakistani societies. Otherwise, irrespective of such jurisdictions, we may identify Muslim society spreading over Asia, Africa and the European segment of Turkey, Jewish society which is not restricted to the state of Israel, Christian society spread all over the world, and so on.

We can employ other directly identifiable criteria but the result will be the same. For example, skin colour differentiates the Whites and the Blacks in the United States of America, and these two communities are identified to form respective societies; but they also constitute American society.

In the same way, a particular objective for its formation may distinguish a society but its constituents would also belong to other kinds of societies. The Asiatic Society of Calcutta or Bombay is constituted of Indians and non-Indians (including non-Asiatics) who have the common objective of advancement of knowledge by means of these societies. However, the members of these societies would not only belong to various other societies identified with reference to their territorial affiliation, political authority, language, religion, skin colour, etc., but may also belong to those societies which have the same or similar objectives—for example, the Royal Asiatic Society in London, the Indian Sociological Society, the Society for the Prevention of Cruelty to Animals, the societies of textile or hardware merchants, to mention a few.

Also, we use omnibus labels, based on distinctive criteria, in order to characterize a society and speak of the capitalist society, feudal society, and so on. Although there is no consensus among social scientists on the definition of 'tribe' or 'elites', for instance, we employ less directly identifiable criteria to characterize a society, such as tribal society, or elite society. All such characteristics of 'society' are not meaningless. They denote society as an entity, but also denote that we cannot understand 'what is society' by means of directly identifiable or any other *external* criteria to characterize them.

These characteristics produce mutually distinct but analogous (i.e., similar or parallel) 'objects'. The 'objects' may retain their *primary* characteristics, like Hindu Bengali society in India *or* Bangladesh, and Muslim Punjabi society in Pakistan *or* India. However, since the primary 'objects' are analogous in nature, they may form their *secondary* composition as Hindu Bengali society in India *and* Bangladesh, and Muslim Punjabi society in Pakistan *and* India. Successively, there would be the possibility of greater composite manifestation of the 'objects' as, say, Hindu and Muslim societies in the world.

Similarly, we can characterize other *sets* of 'society' in terms of the directly identifiable criteria, some of which, in the form of ethnicity, language, religion, political authority, habitation of a common territory, etc., have been brought to account for the examples cited. For instance, we may speak of Christian society in the world or produce a set of 'Christian' societies with reference to the followers of the Syrian Orthodox Church in India, the Coptic Church in Egypt, the Greek Orthodox Church, the Russian Orthodox Church, the Roman Catholic Church, the Protestant Church of various denominations, and so on. We may also employ other external criteria and obtain different sets of 'society', such as the communist societies of the Soviet Union, China, Cuba and Vietnam, or the Communist Party of India, the Communist Party of India (Marxist), and the Communist Party of India (Marxist-Leninist).

Moreover, the same kind of society may be distinguished

by the time variable. Contemporary Bengali society is not the same as it was at the time of Michael Madhusudhan Dutt , Bankim Chandra and Vidyasagar; and both are different from Bengali society at the time of the Sena kings. The Maharashtrian society of today is not the same as at the time of Tilak, and both are different from Maharashtrian society at the time of Shivaji. Rajasthan society in pre-Mughal times was different from the society which emerged during the reigns of Akbar to Aurangzeb, changed again while the Indian Princely States thrived under the suzerainty of the British imperial power, and is surely different today from all those manifestations. Similarly, contemporary English society is not the same as it was in the Victorian era, and the latter was different from English society at the time of Elizabeth I.

Thus, there are considerable variations in space, time and object in conceiving the entity identified as 'society'. In other words, the external criteria for characterizing society denote *variations* in society as an entity, but cannot detect the common thread which binds the variable manifestations of 'society' and thus denote what is society *specifically*.

This is why we find variations in the definition of society in the textbooks on sociology; for the authors emphasize one or some of the above-mentioned or allied criteria and omit others which are equally applicable to the identification of society. We should, therefore, inquire into the *internal conditions* for forming society and determine its existence as an entity. We need to understand in this context the *matrix of variation* (i.e., the mould) in which society is cast while remaining free to change over time and vary according to the place and/or object characteristics.

One may argue that by this procedure we shift our perspective from 'what is society' to 'how does society operate'. Later we shall show that the *what* question is best answered with reference to the *how* question. Therefore, in order to proceed with the matrix of variation, let us pose the *minimax* definition of society: minimally, society is a group constituted of more than one person; maximally, of all human beings.

But, would *any* assortment of two or more persons, or an amorphous assemblage of all human beings constitute society? Obviously it would not. A society does not denote a random collection of persons gathered haphazardly and heedlessly, that is, without a purpose, a perspective, a structure, and the principle to form the structure for the aggregation of people to constitute society. This is exemplified, implicity, by the external characteristics of society we have illustrated. Furthermore, this is why we should next examine the principle—the internal conditions—for constituting 'society', i.e., by proceeding from the minimal condition of considering two or more persons together to the maximum condition which would take into account all the people in the world.

Interactions

When two or more persons are considered together, they must *interact*. Even if two lovers are watching the moon, they are interacting (albeit, neutrally or negatively) by not disturbing each other in the act of watching the moon. They may also interact positively, by holding hands, for instance.

The negative interaction may be as specific as the positive interaction. When two persons are married, they have not only the privilege of interacting sexually but also the obligation of not interacting in that manner with others. This is true as much for those couples who live together without the sacramental or any legal sanction of marriage.

On the other hand, the positive interaction may not always be manifest forcefully, and many even appear to be neutral in character. A Swede father may seem to be unconcerned about the way of life assumed by his children, but not an Indian father. The participation of the Hindus in the public worship of the goddess Durga in Calcutta would appear to be casual in contrast to the Muslim congregation at Calcutta Maidan for the Id prayers. Nevertheless, on both occasions the people would be interacting, and not negatively. The Swede father also may be regarded to interact positively by not interfering in the affairs of his children.

Thus, whether the interactions are negative, neutral, or positive in appearance, we cannot conceive of two or more persons being together without any interaction among them. Therefore, the *first* condition to form 'society' is that its constituents *interact*.

Of course, the interaction between any two persons is primarily personal in nature. Therefore, it may vary interpersonally and the interpersonal relations may persist or disappear. Two lovers may be too ardent, passive but devoted to each other, or they may quarrel and cease to interact as lovers. A married or an unmarried couple may continue to live together, whether or not amicably and, also, whether or not they are faithful to each other; or they may split up. A person may be rigid in maintaining intra-caste and inter-caste interactions, another flexible in that context but within the bounds of caste-wise interactions, while a third may cease to interact within the caste structure of Hindu society. A Muslim or a Hindu may renounce the world and cease to interact with his or her *confrère*, but all *fakirs* and *sanyasis* are not like Kabir or Swami Vivekananda.

However, overriding all such *personal* distinctions, there must be some *commonality* in interactions. If the interpersonal actions were all *unique* in character, the people would have formed a random assortment of interacting individuals in place of all these persons congregating together in a cohesive and concerted manner. This is contrary to our observations and experience in the context of formation of society and its operation as an entity. Even an interaction which appears to be purely personal in character attains a *supra*-personal character in case it is relevant to a *set* of people.

Thus, we are not concerned with the recluses in the Himalayas unless we establish a commonality among them as *sadhus* (holy men) irrespective of the fact that one of them is irascible toward visitors, another is amiable, and the third is indifferent. At the same time, we become concerned with the personal charisma of the respective holy men only when they cease to be recluses and interact in a cohesive and concerted manner with groups of followers. It is from this perspective that we can appreciate the interactions between one who has renounced the world (and is thus beyond 'society') and his or her disciples.

It is clear from this example that irrespective of individual variations, the interactions attain the supra-personal, i.e., the *group* character, in order that society may be formed, operate and exist. This is the *second* condition we should bear in mind for understanding the matrix of variation constituting society as an entity.

As in the case of personalized interactions, group interactions may simultaneously be positive, neutral and negative, and from an additional aspect they may be complementary and contradictory in character. The hippies would react neutrally or negatively to their neighbours but, in a band, they would react positively and complementarily among themselves. A gang of robbers may assume such a negative and contradictory stance that they may even kill others; but among themselves, they must interact positively and complementarily in order to survive as a gang.

As a group, agricultural wage labourers would interact positively and complementarily among themselves, neutrally but complementarily with the group of sharecroppers and other groups of 'rural poor', but negatively and contradictorily with the groups representing vested interests, like the wage labour- or sharecropper-employing landowners, money-lenders, etc.

The complementary interactions among groups, whether or not these are positive or merely neutral in character, would hold the groups together and thus characterize society *in being*. Correspondingly, the contradictory interactions among groups, whether or not these are passively or actively negative in character, would lead toward changes within and between the groups and may cause their ultimate disappearance in order to resolve the contradiction. Society *in becoming* is thus characterized by these group interactions. And, since a set of people simultaneously register a series of complementary and contradictory interactions, society is denoted as an entity, but a *variable* entity.

Thus, because of a series of interactions enacted from the nineteenth century onwards and the interplay of social forces in various ways, with which we need not be presently concerned, caste-wise interactions have been successively modified in contemporary India. However, the complementary caste interactions still override the correspondingly contradictory interactions. Therefore, 'Hindu' society persists while it changes. On the other side, the contradictory interactions between the British and the Indians overpowered the complementary interactions: therefore, in 1947 colonial India was replaced by independent India.

The relative enforcement of the complementary and contradictory group interactions, in the manner we have illustrated, may also lead to the *total* disappearance of a 'society', i.e., of a configuration of world society in terms of specific place, time and people identity. In this case, there may not be a noticeable replacement of one 'society' by another, unlike the one illustrated above. Instead, the 'society' may become extinct, with its residual constituents absorbed in another 'society'. Alternatively, it may merely refer to the elaboration of an extant 'society', or a new 'society' may emerge from the interactions between two (or among a number of) 'societies'.

For example, the Nishada society, which is described as a powerful entity in ancient Indian literature, is said to have been overpowered by the Aryans who settled in India. There is evidence to suggest that the complementary interactions between the Nishadas and the Aryans, at the beginning of contact between the two groups, were later superseded by the contradictory interactions between them. The upshot was that the Nishadas became extinct as a group while those who were left among them were absorbed among the 'untouchables' in Hindu society.

As an example of another possibility we find that Mughal society had at one time occupied the predominant position in the subcontinent of India but was eventually reduced to several components of Muslim society existing in that territory for centuries. In the course of mounting contradictions between the Mughal rulers and the British merchants in India, which increasingly exceeded the complementary interactions established between the two groups from the seventeenth century, Mughal power was ultimately superseded by British power and Mughal society was relegated from its pristine glory to the position of one component of Indian Muslim society, like the Pathans or Sheikhs.

Bengali society, in this context, illustrates how a new 'society' may emerge from the interactions between two (and among a number of) 'societies'. The arboreal economy of Bengal underwent a qualitative change from about the

fifth century AD with the introduction of plough cultivation. As a result, the social structure was transformed
into a caste occupation hierarchy from the conglomeration
of undifferentiated societies of fishermen, rudimentary
agriculturists, food gatherers, etc., which had earlier
maintained some sort.of coexistence in that territory. The
importation of *Brahmanadharma* (the religion of the
Brahmans) at the same time had a significant role to play
in this course of transformation of several tribal societies
into a component of Hindu society. The new mode of production and the lifestyle of the Hindus established more
extensive and intensive complementary group interactions among the autochthones, and the contradictory
group interactions which had emerged with the immig-
rants, at the beginning, were soon overpowered. Bengali
society thus emerged in the subcontinent of India.

On a global scale, however, the complementary group
interactions cannot *totally* override the contradictory
group interactions, and vice versa. The first eventuality
would reduce human society to a state of *static equilibrium*
which is belied by our experience. For, however slowly or
rapidly, all societies identified as entities are seen to
change over the three dimensions of variation in the
place (*sthāna*), the time (*kāla*), and the object or people
(*pātra*), as it has been delineated in Hindu philosophy. On
the other side, the second eventuality would nullify the
existence of human society by the *total* destruction of all
group interactions on a global scale. Therefore, between
these two extreme and unreal eventualities, world society
remains in a state of *dynamic equilibrium*, i.e., its various
configurations maintain their identities at a *point* in time
and change within or between themselves over a *period* of
time.

For example, in one of the smallest groupings in world
society, viz., the family forming a co-resident and commensal kin group, both complementary and contradictory

interactions are noticeable. In a joint family these interactions must take the group character between and within the generation levels as, say, among the sibling couples in each generation. From this point of reference, in case the contradictory interactions override the corresponding complementary interactions, the sibling couples (with their respective progeny) separate from one another. A three-generation collateral joint family at a point in time may thus turn into several unilineal joint families of procreation of the siblings now located at the top-most generation level of each family. This will happen because the contradictory interactions between the families of procreation of these siblings would supersede the complementary interactions within the collateral joint family of orientation previously maintained by the same siblings. In the same manner, a unilineal joint family of procreation, at a point in time, turns into several nuclear families when the siblings located at the lower generation level separate with their consorts and children. Other variations may also take place from a basic joint family organization over a time period.

Similar changes in the immediately identifiable configuration of world society may be seen in the historical context. For example, the contradictory group interactions between the English and Scottish societies exceeded the corresponding complementary interactions in the time of Elizabeth I. The relative alignments of the two kinds of interactions, however, changed over time and British society emerged in due course. Yet, the rival identities of English and Scottish societies have not totally lost their relevance in the time of Elizabeth II.

The contradictory group interactions may have a more lasting effect and override the complementary group interactions established at successive points in time. For example, by exceeding their complementary aspect, the contradictory group interactions changed the configuration of Indian society and replaced it in 1947 by two configurations of Indian and Pakistani societies. Successively, by exceeding their complementary aspect, the contradictory group interactions between East and the West Pakistanis led in 1971 to the emergence of a third configuration in the form of Bangladeshi society in the subcontinent of India.

Societies may thus change their form and/or content, but the contradictory group interactions cannot display any cancerous condition toward obliterating world society. As illustrated, one society may become extinct, another may be dovetailed into an extant society, the third may emerge out of several societies, or the newly emerged societies may attest to coexistence at a point in time while bearing the possibility of changing over time. For instance, we should take note of both sides of the fact that, contemporarily, the complementary (or neutral) group interactions prevail over the contradictory group interactions among Indian, Pakistani, and Bangladeshi societies, and of all of them with the 'master society' of the British in pre-1947 days. Nonetheless, further alienation from, or consolidation of, these societies in the subcontinent of India cannot be ruled out in future.

However, all such changes can occur within and between the configurations of world society which will persist so long as humans exist. We are, therefore, led to the conclusion that the static and the dynamics of society as a variable entity refer to the relative alignments of the complementary (positive or neutral) and the contradictory (or negative) group interactions within and between each and every configuration of world society: the configurations identified by the place, time and object dimensions of variation. This means that the matrix of variation for understanding society is finally conditioned by the relative magnitude of the forces generated by the complementary and contradictory group interactions.

When the two gamuts of forces, generated respectively by the complementary and contradictory group interactions, balance each other within a range of tolerance, the configuration of society—in which the gamuts operate—retains its character while maintaining its existence. When, on the other hand, the gamut of forces generated by the contradictory group interactions exceeds that generated by the complementary group interactions, changes take place in the character of the configuration and these changes may ultimately lead to the total disappearance of that configuartion of society or its replacement by another. The former condition thus denotes society *in being*, the latter *in becoming*.

Now, in order to appraise the relative magnitude of the two gamuts of forces, we should first ascertain the structure of their operation. This requires a conceptual frame which we shall discuss, next, in a schematic sequence of constructing the operative structure.

Social Action

Interaction (i.e., action and reaction) presupposes the intention and awareness of the interacting persons regarding how to act and how to react. The act of slapping a 'friend' on the back is reacted to by the return of a 'friendly' back-slap or a smile or some such gesture. But the same action from an 'enemy' would be reacted to differently, such as, with a punch on the nose. Correspondingly, the same action from a totally unfamiliar person would put one in a quandary: should the reaction be amicable or antagonistic, or none at all? Obviously, in the last case, the *meaning* of interaction is absent unlike in the former two cases. Therefore, there may be no reaction or a reaction of a random (i.e., not consistent) character.

As noted earlier, for the same kind of interaction the exact action and reaction of the interacting individuals would vary. However, it would vary within the limit set by the meaning of the interaction. The 'friendly' interaction need not be limited to back-slapping, the 'enemy-like' interaction need not always be violent. But the commonality (and, thus, the consistency) of the interaction would be conveyed by the meaning attributed to it as being friendly or enemy-like. Because this commonality is missing when an unfamiliar person slaps one on the back, one cannot read the meaning of the act and react accordingly.

All this means that any interaction must have meanings behind it. One acts with a particular purpose in mind and one reacts with a particular purpose in mind.

The purpose, however, may or may not be the same for two actors. A 'friendly' act of the kind cited above may be interpreted as an 'unfriendly' act by the person acted upon, and vice versa. The reaction would accordingly be different. But, if most of the actions and reactions of individuals were uncertain in character, there could not be any commonality in interactions. As a result, there would either have been no interaction or it would be at random, as in the case of an act with an unfamiliar person. This means that without conveying *sustained* meanings as the result of specific purposes behind them, the interactions cannot be the principle for structuring the matrix of variation to denote society.

The sustained meanings of interactions would, of course, be different as the *nature* of the purpose behind the actions and reactions of interacting persons is different. When the purpose is the same, complementary interaction is recorded. When the purpose is different, contradictory interaction would be recorded. For example, when one boards a bus, the conductor acts by demanding passage fare from that person. The person may react by paying the fare and, thus, by meeting the expectations of the conductor's action record a complementary interaction. Alternatively, the person may refuse to pay because of a protest movement against raising bus fare and, thus, record a contradictory interaction with the bus conductor.

In this context, the personalized interaction of the bus conductor and the passenger is of no concern to us. The conductor may be polite or rude in asking for the fare, and so might be the passenger while paying or not paying the fare. These variations would be examined in the context of the psychology of individuals. Also, as noted earlier, we shall not be concerned with the complementary or contradictory interactions of individuals in order to understand society so long as these are of random occurrence; for neither of the two would then register any sustained meaning.

Interactions are, thus, seen to convey sustained meanings of one kind or the other when they are *repetitive*. To pursue the example cited above, when a person repeatedly refuses to pay the fare while riding a bus, we definitely regard him or her as a 'deviant' in society (whether or not the deviation is desirable or undesirable for the future of society) because this does not conform to the complementary interactions of other passengers who pay the demanded fare with the bus conductor.

In the above example the implication is that the 'social' meaning acquired by the deviant reaction of an individual may assume group character, just as the passengers paying the fare to the owners of the transport service (through the media of bus conductors) register a group-wise complementary interaction. For example, as a protest against a rise in bus fare, some passengers may come together as a group and demand in a cohesive manner to ride the bus but not pay the enhanced fare. This will be regarded as a 'social' event while the contradictory group interaction may lead to a clash and result in burning buses.

Of course, interaction of this form cannot be repeated *ad infinitum* unless the transport system in society is allowed to be totally disrupted. If that system is to be maintained, either the enhanced bus fare would be withdrawn or the recalcitrant group of passengers would in some way be coerced to react by paying the increased bus fare. The complementary group interaction would thus be restored by resolving the contradictory group interaction in the form of either a reversal to a *status quo ante* or the emergence of a new social situation.

Thus, when interactions convey distinctive meanings and are also repetitive in character, they acquire a 'social' (and not merely a personal) relevance. Therefore, in sociology, meaningfully repetitive interactions are called *social actions*. The label of social action was particularly favoured by Max Weber. It has, however, gained a general acceptance as it forms the base of the structure we require for conceiving the matrix of variation in society.

The formulation is valid even though the same action may refer to two different kinds of reaction by conveying respective meanings. For example, definitely up to the last generation and frequently in this generation as well, an elder in the kinship network of the Hindus (as also of the Muslims) would extend his feet to be touched by the younger ones as a form of salutation. On the other hand, a person who wants his footwear polished will also extend his feet to a shoeshine boy, irrespective of differences between the two in religion, caste and age. However, the meanings conveyed by the same action are different. Therefore, the reaction in the former case would be honouring the elder kin member and, in the latter case, a monetary transaction in the service sector of the society's economy. We would thus be concerned with two different kinds of social action while proceeding from the same action.

The formulation of social action is also relevant to those cases in which an action appears to have no purpose behind it or appears not to anticipate a reaction. To illustrate first with reference to an individual, as we have done so far, a student may stop reading his or her textbook and look at the sky for a while. This may be a stray instance, or it may be repeated because the student's mind is wandering away from the textbooks as he or she is fatigued by reading for a long time or is in the grip of some other interest. In either case, the action of not reading the textbook has a purpose behind it, and there must be a reaction—whether or not that reaction is complementary or contradictory. For instance, the reaction could be that the student recovers from fatigue or the extraneous distraction and, thus, registers a complementary reaction to reading. Alternatively, the student may register a contradictory reaction by discontinuing to read altogether.

Such personal interactions assume a social character when they turn into meaningfully repetitive interactions and are transformed, on that basis, into group interactions. Therefore, there are topics for research in the forms of sociology of work and fatigue, sociology of leisure, sociology of youth or students' unrest, and so on.

The concept of social action is equally applicable to those interactions which may not be caused by one's own volition. These interactions are imputed to be ordained supernaturally or considered inevitable owing to the objective conditions and the inexorable course of history. However, the meaningfully repetitive interactions—forming group interactions eventually—can vary as complementary (positive or neutral) and contradictory (or negative) in character.

For example, according to a common belief in Indian society (as also in many societies in the world), it is fate which ultimately decides how one acts and reacts. This is imputed in the role of *niyati* as described in the Hindu epics, Ramayana and Mahabharata. All the same, meaningfully repetitive interactions do take place in society, which are particularly underlined by the role of *purusakara* (achievement) as opposed to *niyati* (fate). We may recall the instances of interactions between the Kauravas and the Pandavas, and with their allies, in the Mahabharata—which are particularly highlighted by the meaningfully repetitive interactions between Karna and Arjuna.

Objective and historical circumstances force one to act and react so that interaction in this context invariably assumes a group character. But the nature of interaction may vary. For example, the interactions between zamindars (landlords) and ryots (peasants with tenancy rights), which emerged from the British enactment of the Permanent Settlement of Land in 1793, became objectively and historically redundant in Indian society with the commodification of crop and the consequent emergence (or prevalence) of interactions between the non-cultivating (but farm-holding) landowners and the landless (or semi-landless) sharecroppers and farm labourers. However, the zamindars acted and reacted concertedly to *resist* the change in the objective and historical circumstances, or to *comply* with it (and thus try to neutralize the change) by turning themselves into sharecropper- and wage labour-employing landholders. Also, some of them *pursued* the change positively by removing themselves from any form of land-based interaction. Distinctive changes in group interactions were thus registered in Indian society from the 1930s and in the 1950s in particular.

The role of social action, as we have just illustrated, is clearly underlined by Karl Marx and Frederick Engels, although they are often accused of believing in fatalistic 'economic determinism'. Marx's assertion, that 'in the social production of their life, men enter into definite relations that are indispensable and independent of their will', (Marx 1951: I. 328) was substantiated by Engels when he wrote that 'men make their history themselves, only they do so in a given environment which conditions it and on the basis of actual relations already existing ' (Engels 1951: II. 458).

Thus, from all perspectives—the idealist, existentialist, materialist, and so on—social action is seen to provide the *base* of the structure which denotes the matrix of variation or the mould for the understanding of society.

Social Behaviour

At any point in time and place, there would be several social actions between two persons. In India, as in other configurations of world society, a father and a son interact in meaningfully repetitive but various ways. The perennial affection and concern of the father for his son, his responsibility and duties to look after him when he is young, and his expectation of privileges and the right to be looked after by the son when he himself is old, are translated into a multitude of meaningful actions. The son's actions will have to be complementary and meaningful if the father and the son are to interact in a sustained manner.

These meaningfully repetitive and sustained social actions between a father and a son may vary in many ways, although we may restrict our attention to a specific place and a particular time. It is frequently found in contemporary India that while the father had felt obligated to look after his own father in his old age, his son does not feel in the same way. Therefore, the father in the present generation renounces (resentfully or not) any meaningful action to be looked after by his son in his old age. At the same time and at the same place, another set of father and son may maintain the understanding of looking after the young and being looked after in old age, so that the envisaged *totality* of social actions between the father and the son would not be impaired. Also, a father with several sons may exhibit the totality of social actions with one or a few of them, but not all. The nature and the degree of curtailment of the gamut of social actions between the father and the son(s) would thus vary.

The social actions between father and son may vary in many other ways. For instance, under the prevailing circumstances in India, the son may 'grow up' at a younger age than his father did a generation earlier. His father's reciprocally meaningful actions relating to his duties toward his son may accordingly be less in number or intensity than were his own father's toward him. Further, this may not be true for another set of father and son in present-day India, while these differences may be noticed with reference to particular sons of the same father.

Thus we find that we must be concerned with a number of social actions for *one set* of interacting persons, although we have deliberately chosen an easily comprehensible set between father and son, examined the set under the most simplified situation of only two interacting persons denoted as a father and his son, and negelcted any major variation by the time and the place of occurrence of these social actions in order to avoid complications. Even so, we notice that we must not only deal with an envisaged totality of social actions but this gamut of social actions too is liable to variation.

Similar totalities of social actions and their possibility of variation can be envisaged for more and more complex sets of interacting persons. Proceeding from father and son, we may consider the interacting group as composed of parents and children, grandparents and grandchildren, uncles/aunts and nephews/nieces, and so on. Of these three interacting groups, the first would be the least complex and the third the most.

The parents would be of one kind only, with the internal distinction of being father and mother; and the children, distinguished as sons and daughters, would correspondingly be of one kind. The grandparents would be of two kinds as father's parents and mother's parents, and so would be the grandchildren as sons' children and daughters' children. The uncles and aunts would be of four kinds, each distinguished by sex as: father's brother and father's sister, mother's brother and mother's sister, father's brother's wife and father's sister's husband, and mother's brother's wife and mother's sister's husband. Correspondingly, the nephews and nieces would be of four kinds while further variations may be noticed among the four kinds of avunuclar interactions. For example, the interaction with his nephew or niece would be different for a father's elder and younger brother in a Hindu family, the mother's brother plays a crucial role among some African people, but all the four kinds would be treated equally in European and American societies.

These and allied sets of interactions (e.g., among siblings or siblings-in-law) can be considered in a wider coverage, namely, as interactions within a family or a kin group formed by blood relatives (kin) and relatives by marriage of one's own or of the blood relatives (affines). We may also consider more complicated sets of interactions than those within the circuit in which a person is born, viz., the family and the kin group.

Interactions within and between castes are not concerned solely with the issue of purity and pollution. A multitude of social actions, spreading beyond pollution, commensality and connubium, register caste identities and inter-caste distances.

All are equal before God, according to Islam (which,

incidentally, is the message of virtually all religions). However, Muslim society in the subcontinent of India is hierarchically structured by the Mughals, Pathans, Sayyads, Sheikhs, the sects of Khojas, Bohras, etc., and the 'functional castes' of weavers, oil-pressers, etc. Networks of social actions govern these identities and their respective distances in the social hierarchy.

Interactions within and between landowning and landless interests in India (or, for that matter, in any configuration of world society) are not merely with reference to agricultural production and distribution. A multitude of social actions related to the 'economic' and other aspects of their life registers the identities and distinctions as wage labourers, sharecroppers, marginal peasants, labour-employing farmers, and sharecropper-employing landholders.

Similarly, the interactions within and between the workers, executives and management in an industrial concern are not restricted to the social actions related to the jobs performed. These interactions reflect political and other connotations and register a specific totality of social actions. The role of multinationals, spread virtually all over the world, has given a global dimension to these interactions.

Ethnicity, which refers to the ethos—'the characteristic spirit' of a community of people—is not expressed anywhere in the world merely in the mental horizon of the persons concerned. It refers to a network of social actions which assert ethnic solidarity and inter-ethnic distinctions, or forego that distinction. Of the former, the 'unrests' prevailing in eastern India from the time of independence or the Jharkhand Movement are telling examples. Of the latter we find an example in the course of the merger of the Lepchas of Darjeeling with the Nepali community.

On a global scale, political considerations alone do not signify the totalities of social actions within and between the nation-states. The European Common Market, the 'dependency' of one nation-state upon another, *détente* between the Great Powers, etc., subsume various meta-political social actions in world society.

In sum, multitudes of mutually distinct but analogous or homologous sets of social actions record identities, distinctions and interrelations among all kinds of groupings in world society. These groups are formed by individuals according to their *ascription* to the world society in being through the media of family, kinship, caste, religion, ethnicity, and so on. These groups are also formed by *achievement* in the world society in being and becoming through the media of occupational, educational, political, and such other choice bodies. Finally, these groups are formed by ascription or achievement in the world system perspective of social dynamism through the media of nation-states; internationalization of the nation-states into the First, the Second and the Third Worlds; international division of labour; various forms of territorial, cultural and such other agglomerations like the Latin Americans, Asians and Arabs, Whites-Blacks-Hispanics, and Orientals and Occidentals.

In all these cases the totalities of social actions—with the possibility of variation within the totalities—may be comprehended only if the respective sets of social actions are sustained and do not occur sporadically. Our day-to-day observations and experience in any configuration of world society substantiate this point and denote thereby that there is an understanding within and between the respectively interacting groups for meaningfully repetitive social actions: from those between a father and a son in perhaps the simplest unit of parents and children to those between world communities.

Now, how does this understanding emerge and operate? Obviously this cannot be a spontaneous phenomenon, just as social actions are not spontaneous 'individual actions'. The understanding may emerge only from the meaning repeatedly conveyed by means of the social action to each other (or one another) in an interacting group. It is also implied that the understanding can operate only when the social actions are repeated and sustained. This means that the understanding evolves through a process of learning which is commonly described as *socialization*. In this process the respective gamuts of social actions are the initiators and also the products in the sense that these gamuts anticipate the expected *behaviour* of the interacting persons.

Personal and individual behaviour thus attain a 'social' character by representing a particular set of social actions. In the sociological literature, therefore, this form of behaviour is denoted as *social behaviour*.

Conceived in this manner, social behaviour may determine within a range of flexibility the interactions of persons who are not directly in contact or meet in an unprecedented situation. For example, a middle class resident of Calcutta or Bombay may not have met a cultivator but, if he does, his behaviour toward the latter is likely to be condescending in character as befitting the envisaged social behaviour between a Babu (gentleman) and a *chasi* (peasant). Otherwise, if the Babu is surcharged with the emotional or ideological meaning of equality, he would behave toward the cultivator as a *chasi bhai* (peasant brother) which may not reduce the anticipated behavioural distance between the gentry and the folk.

Corresponding interactions between a White and a Black in a nation-state (e.g., the USA) or beyond the nation-state (e.g., between the Euro-Americans and the Afro-Asians) are not unknown. These interactions reflect the social behaviour of ethnocentrism or other forms of socialization which anticipate behavioural distance or equality irrespective of the fact that the interacting persons may or may not meet.

If we now recall the example of interaction between two unfamiliar persons which would be of a random nature unless their behaviour pattern is anticipated, we would appreciate how such interactions also fall within the matrix of variation for understanding society. The unfamiliar persons will interact in terms of the anticipated behaviour pattern they had learnt through the process of socialization.

Rabindranath Tagore had thus spoken of the 'petty' and the 'grand' Englishmen (*chhoto o boro*) and differentiated the former from the latter in terms of their expected behaviour in the Crown Colony of India of looking down upon the 'natives': a course of socialization from which the 'grand' Englishmen at home were spared. We may also recall that barring the minority of 'grand Englishmen', the anticipated behaviour pattern between the masters and the subjects had largely determined the social behaviour of the British toward the Indians, and vice versa, whether or not a British worker and an Indian peasant had ever met.

As in the case of social action, social behaviour also changes in its form and content. The course of change is registered as certain social actions depicting the behaviour pattern are withdrawn, replaced, or newly enforced. Any one of these possibilities may occur whether or not the interacting persons are in physical contact, as attested to by the change in the form and the content of the pattern of behaviour between the British and the Indians from the pre-independence era of India's history to date.

Similarly, with reference to a perennial contact of the interacting persons we find that a new form of social behaviour has emerged between the landowning and the landless interests in India, with the disappearance of the social actions between the zamindars and the *ryots*, and their partial replacement by the social actions between the non-cultivating landowners and the sharecroppers and agricultural wage labourers. In this form of social behaviour, the *contractual* rather than the *customary* social actions are increasingly manifest as its content.

We also find that while in the smallest unit of father-son interactions the behaviour pattern is becoming less and less 'authoritative-submissive' and more and more 'friendly', the intra-caste and the inter-caste behaviour patterns are changing as depicted by the disappearance, replacement and new enforcement of a number of social actions. The social behaviour of the occupational and political groups is becoming similar all over the world. Also, along with the replacement of the social behaviour of the monopoly capitalists in the domineering nation-states by that of the multinationals, the slogan of 'workmen of all countries, unite!' has presently attained an international behavioural meaning in the context of the international division of labour. Needless to say, the interacting groups in these contexts may not meet perennially or at all.

Thus, through direct and indirect and casual or sustained interactions, social behaviour encompasses entire humanity. This accounts for the oft-repeated cliche: Man is a social animal. It signifies that society in being may be depicted by the existing network of social behaviour, and the society in becoming may correspondingly be depicted by changes in that network. While the relevance of this formulation in sciencing society will be examined later, suffice it to say for the present that it is with reference to social behaviour that we may appreciate the nature and the course of variation in social actions: past, present and potential. Therefore, for the construction of the mould to understand society, social behaviour stands next in sequence to social action which, as noted, provides the base of the conceptual frame.

Social Relationship

Social behaviour of any kind, depicting a set of social actions, operates between two terminal points, such as, father and son, two members of one caste or religion, two members of different castes or religion, and two citizens of the same or different nation-states. Thus, a dyadic relationship is envisaged with reference to the operation of social behaviour and social action. However, this dyadic relationship is not person-specific. We are not presently concerned with a particular father and a particular son, but with *clusters* of fathers and sons.

The father-son relationship denotes one kind of social behaviour while the familial relationships within and between families denote collections of different kinds of social behaviour. However, each collection forms a *homologous* (common) multitude, and the multitudes are *analogous* (parallel) for the respective collections. Also, the multitudes or the respective kinds of social behaviour denote, in their sequence, specific gamuts of social actions.

Similarly, when we consider the relationship within a caste, it is not with respect to any two specific caste members but among all caste members in the cluster. Inter-caste relationship refers to any member in one caste and any member in another caste, or any member in the respective castes forming a set of clusters. And so it is with respect to the relationships within and between religions, nation-states, and so on.

In all these cases we *deduce* a common form of social behaviour—depicting a specific set of *observable* social actions—among the individuals in a cluster or the individuals belonging to two or more parallel clusters. The dyadic relationship within a cluster or between the clusters thus expresses a reciprocally sustained meaning to hold them together. By attaining a supra-personal character, this relationship is therefore labelled *social relationship*.

The terminal points to denote a social relationship form a set of clusters which may subdivide a set of bigger clusters or cut across another set of clusters. The Hindus and Muslims all over the world form two clearly distinguished clusters while the Shias, Sunnis, Khojas, Bohras, etc., form sub-clusters within the Muslim cluster, and the Vaishnavas, Saktas, Lingayats, etc., form sub-clusters among the Hindus. Father and mother register the conjugal relationship, the sons and daughters the sibling relationship; but by cutting across the parental-filial relationship, father and children register the paternal-filial relationship and mother and children the maternal-filial relationship. The Indian Bangladeshi relationship cuts across their intra-ethnic relationship as Bengali and also ignores their clustering by Hindu-Muslim relationship. The bourgeois-proletarian relationship can be envisaged as forming two clusters within a nation-state or internationally by cutting across the nation-state boundaries.

Thus, by forming clusters in various ways and each cluster expressing a distinctively repetitive meaning, the social relationships form a network for understanding society at a point in time, i.e., at the state of society in being.

However, each social relationship would vary as the multitude of social behaviour it expresses (and, correspondingly, the gamuts of social action depicted by the multitude) would vary. But these variations must be within the limits of sustaining the relationships. Familial actions and behaviour change and are expressed by changes in familial relationships. For example, it is said that the father-son relationship in contemporary India is less 'authoritative-submissive' and more 'friendly' than before. We have noted changes in the social behaviour and the social actions between father and son in this context. However, we should also note that these changes are within the limits of sustaining the relationship. Otherwise, they would be ludicrous if the father-son relationship is not to be retained, as portrayed in Aldous Huxley's *Brave New World*.

Similarly, Hindu–Muslim riots in India, Pakistan, or Bangladesh disrupt the actions and behaviour perennially present between the two communities. The abnormal situation thus created affects the sustained meaning of Hindu–Muslim relationships within these nation-states and also between them. Nonetheless, so long as these disruptions are transitory and do not lead to a decisive rupture in the previously sustained actions and behaviour, the Hindu–Muslim relationship does not disappear from the social scene.

Over a time period, however, a social relationship may undergo qualitative change when the multitude of social behaviour it expresses (and the corresponding sets of social action it depicts) undergoes a qualitative change. The relationships among the Hindu *varnas* of Brahman, Kshatriya, Vaishya, and Shudra are not merely the consolidation of relationships among the *jatis*, although virtually all *jatis* are affiliated to one or other *varna* in contemporary India and the *jati* division of Hindu society is accepted to have emerged after the Aryans settled in India and exhibited the *varna* division of society. Therefore, caste relations are expressed by the multitude of social behaviour (and the gamuts of social action) within and between the *jatis* which is not merely an elaboration of the social behaviour and social actions relevant to the relationships within and between the *varnas*.

A social relationship may also disappear totally if the gamuts of social action and the multitude of social behaviour which expresses that relationship disappear. The avuncular relationship commands more respectful behaviour than that toward a senior cousin. This is substantiated for Indian society in which the distinction is consistently maintained irrespective of the degree of distance within and between the two relationships, such as, between father's brother and father's father's brother's son (= uncle one degree apart) or between father's brother's son (first degree cousin) and father's father's brother's son's son (= second degree cousin). But the distinction is lost to Anglo-American society for the avuncular relationship several degrees apart, and these uncles and aunts are addressed and treated as 'cousins'.

On the other hand, a parallel kind of social behaviour (and the corresponding social actions) may emerge and denote a parallel relationship. The caste system does not function in the United States, but when one speaks of the caste of Boston Brahmins one refers to caste-like social behaviour of superiority and self-imposed isolation from the others in society as in the case of Hindu Brahmins. A distinct kind of social relationship in a casteless society is thus expressed.

However, all previous social relationships cannot just disappear and new relationships emerge in a vacuum. Usually, therefore, one relationship is *replaced* by another which expresses a different multitude of social behaviour and the corresponding gamuts of social action. This is seen with reference to what is known as 'social mobility' along a status hierarchy, which is frequently equated to changes in the prestige scale of occupations placed in a hierarchy from the lowest to the highest in a configuration of world society. It is also evident in the world perspective of resolution of contradictory social relationships and the replacement of the previously operating ones by a more complementary set.

In case a cultivator's son is able to secure a clerical job and thus 'promote' himself to Babu status, the *chasi*-Babu relationship would be replaced by the relationship between Babus. Alternatively, if a Babu takes to the vocation of a mechanic and thus 'demotes' himself in social status by performing a manual job, the Babu-worker relationship would be replaced by the relationship among workers. In both cases, the nuances of previous relationships would linger for a while and the behaviour patterns would not be exactly the same as among well-established Babus or workers. But that would be a passing phenomenon because consensus must prevail, amidst changes, for society to exist. Thus, by meeting the aspirations and the limitations of the people, society for its existence over time is structured more and more harmoniously and efficiently by the replacement of social relationships.

The Marxists would not agree to an ahistorical assertion of the existentialists and the ideologue that because of the need of the people to exist 'socially' or to fulfil their spiritual needs one set of social relationships is replaced by another. By emphasizing the issue of conflict as against consensus, they would argue that the social relationships which become contradictory to the inexorable course of history must eventually be replaced by more complementary relationships and, thus, society is structured more and more harmoniously and efficiently. This will be pointed out in terms of the replacement of customary feudal relationships by the bourgeois contractual relationships, and in terms of the replacement of the contradictory capital-labour relationship in bourgeois society by the socialized capital-labour relationship. Nevertheless, in order to examine all these viewpoints regarding society in becoming, one's attention is drawn to the conceptualization of social relationship as a landmark in the frame of reference for understanding society.

We may note the basic agreement on the concept of social relationship despite the opposite views held by scholars on consensus or conflict for ensuring social dynamism, with which the names of Max Weber and Karl Marx are commonly associated. In the words of Max Weber, a social relationship expresses 'the behaviour of a plurality of actors in so far as, in its manifest content, the action of each takes account of that of the others and is oriented in those terms'(1947: 107). In the words of Karl Marx, by social relationship 'we understand the cooperation of several individuals, no matter under what conditions, in what manner and to what end' (1942: 18).

Thus, irrespective of the difference in scholarly perspectives, while social behaviour has been shown to encompass humanity, it is manifest because of (and according to) the social relationships drawn between the directly and indirectly interacting persons and groups serving as the reference points.

However, a social relationship is neither a matter of observation, although people state the relationship, nor is it a matter of deduction from the relational terms. In these two respects, a social relationship is different from social action on the one hand and social behaviour on the other. It is a matter of *interpretation* to 'expound the meaning' of a gamut of observable social actions and the corresponding set of deducible social behaviour. This point needs to be explained in some detail.

An aged woman may be addressed as 'mother', but without drawing the same relationship as one would draw with one's actual mother. Consequently, one will register different kinds of social behaviour with the 'aged woman' and the actual mother, although there may be similarities in the two behaviour patterns. Correspondingly, the respective

77

gamuts of social actions will be different. Therefore, a distinction has been drawn in sociological literature between sociocentric and egocentric kinship relations.

The term for a relationship may also be used in totally different contexts, such as, 'brother-in-law' (*sālā*) in Indian or 'sister' in American slang. When a *chasi* is addressed as *chasi-bhai*, he is not really treated as 'brother'. On the other hand, slogans like 'Hindi-Chini Bhaibhai' or 'Hindi-Russi Bhaibhai' might have been meant for such a treatment in the sociocentric perspective. A relational term may also acquire an omnibus meaning, for instance, when the womenfolk are eulogized as *matrijati* (the 'mother' sector of humankind), or when the word 'comrade' is employed in a 'friendly' or jocular manner for all and sundry (i.e., without its connotation in political economy).

We arrive, therefore, at the following generalization with respect to the operative principles of social action, social behaviour and social relationship, which form a sequence for understanding society as it exists at a point in time and as it changes over a period in time.

1. Any interaction among individuals is *spontaneously observable*. Social action, however, is a matter of *sustained observation*.

2. Social behaviour appears to be observable from the actions and reactions of individuals located within a group or under mutually distinguished groups. In fact, it is a matter of *deduction* from the observable gamuts of social actions.

3. A social relationship seems to be given in a place-, time- and people-bound configuration of human society or in world society at large. In point of fact, however, the relationship is a matter of *interpretation* from the deduced behaviour patterns which, in turn, are ascertained from the observable multitude of social actions.

We should also bear in mind that the interpretation of social relationship is essential for understanding the statics and dynamics of society, viz., the society in being and becoming. Thus, social relationships compose the third tier of the conceptual frame of reference for understanding society, of which the first two tiers are social action and social behaviour, respectively.

Social Institutions

People can state their social relationships because each relationship expresses the particular way in which they are consolidated in society. At the same time, a social relationship is a matter of interpretation because it refers to the purpose of the consolidation of people in various ways. This formulation may appear confusing. However, the confusion can be cleared by conceptualizing the source of stating and interpreting social relationships; for, social relaitonships emerge from those agencies in society which prompt individuals to interact repetitively in a meaningful manner and sustain these interactions in order to denote specific behaviour patterns.

The agencies have emerged, and continue to emerge, because of the necessity for human beings to live together under specified terms and conditions. The agencies also promote and regulate people's desire to live differently from the manner in which they had lived at a previous time period. As a result, while some social actions, social behaviour and social relationships disappear, emerge anew, or are replaced over time, the society continues to exist and operate. We may briefly examine some of these agencies, each of which implies a specific set of privileges and obligations, rights and duties, of the interacting persons.

Society cannot exist without the reproduction of its constituents, but the process of reproduction needs to be regulated. Failing this, society would disintegrate from the sexual tension generated in it or from the consequences of sexual reproduction. Promiscuity in sexual union was hypothesized at the earliest stage of formation of human society, and sexual union of a group of men with a group of women at the next stage. The information cited as evidence of the successive stages of promiscuity and group marriage has been discounted by many, just as monogamy being the earliest regulated form of sexual union has been questioned. We find, however, that a man and a woman may have a stable sexual union strictly between the two (monogamy), whether or not they undergo sacred or secular rites to inaugurate this course of regulated social actions, social behaviour and social relationship. Equally, a man may have a stable sexual union with a number of women (polygyny) or a woman may have the same with a number of men (polyandry).

The pattern of such social action, social behaviour and social relationship may change as one form of sexual union is superseded by another: the change being voluntary or induced for the people concerned. For example, in the first half of the 19th century, Pandit Iswar Chandra Vidyasagar of Bengal organized a movement to enact laws for the prohibition of polygyny among the Hindus, but he was not successful. The law was enacted in the Republic of India in the 1950s, but the practice had virtually been abandoned by that time, as is seen from population census data.

However, the sexual union of men and women is regulated in one form or another, although the form may vary over place and time. Even companiate marriage, which is becoming increasingly popular in Euro-American society, is subject to a series of voluntarily accepted rights and duties between the man and the woman. An agency is thus at work to promote and regulate the privileges and obligations, the rights and duties, of the sexually interacting persons in society. This agency we know as the *institution* of marriage.

Marriage produces the identitiy of children born to their parents, and enjoins upon them the obligation and duty to rear the children and the privilege and right(?) to be maintained by the children in their old age. The identity of children for this course of social action, behaviour and relationship is not, however, purely biological. Putative parenthood is known in virtually all configurations of world society.

The Hindu law-givers were concerned with the regulation of sexual union in society and the consequent 'purity' of the children born. Nonetheless, they mention those sons who are not biologically related to their father: the *kanina*, the *sahoda*, the *gudhaja*, etc. Moreover, renowned law-givers like Kautliya and Manu condemned or tried to prohibit widow marriage (viz., the Arthashastra and the Manusmrti), but they stipulated that in case a widow wished to have a son under the paternity of her deceased husband, she could undergo the ritual of *niyoga* with another man and produce a *kshetraja* son. A man who was unable to procreate but desired to continue his lineage could have sons by his wife or wives by following the custom of *niyoga*, i.e., by employing specific person(s) for the purpose. In one version of the Ramayana, Rama and his three brothers are implied by this procedure to be the sons of King Dasharatha, just as the five Pandavas of the Mahabharata are Kunti's and Madri's *niyoga* sons and Kunti's first son Karna is a *kanina* son. It is worth noting in the present context that as Karna was reared in the family of a *suta* (chariot-maker by *jati* nomenclature) from the time of his birth, he was identified all through his life as a *sutaputra* (son of a *suta*).

It is thus evident from various sources (and many more may be enumerated) that from the moment a person is born, his or her privileges and obligations, rights and duties, are *socially* determined with reference to the 'family': another social institution.

Simultaneously, the person's social relationships (and the consequent social behaviour and social actions) with others in society are determined by virtue of his or her birth. The determining agencies are 'ascriptive' to him or her, and refer to such institutions as kinship, caste, religion, ethnicity, or citizenship. The person may denounce the ascriptive agencies at a later age and, thus, renounce the corresponding social relationships, behaviour and actions. Nevertheless, from birth certain kinds of social behaviour (and the corresponding social actions) are learnt by the person in terms of the social relationships he or she draws through the ascriptive social institutions.

Then there are the institutions with which a person is connected in later life in order to interact with other members in society. The person thus draws various forms of 'achieved' social relationships with reference to education, economic activities, political pursuits, recreational agencies, spiritual quest, etc. Education calls for the social relationships within and between the teachers and the students, and, more recently, many other ancillary relationships with reference to the organization of educational activities by means of schools, colleges, universities, vocational training centres, apprenticeship, etc. Economic activities immediately produce relationships within and between the occupational groups while the relations of production yield the classes as conceived by Karl Marx. The political pursuits lead to various social relationships among those in power, those striving for power, and between the Establishment and the Opposition. The recreational agencies can produce even violent group interactions, as we find in many places in India with respect to 'sporting clubs'. The spiritual quest, be it religious or purely philosophical, yields a 'fraternal' relationship among the disciples, a 'paternal' relationship with the *gurus* (masters), and so on.

There are also other activities associated with the life and living of a person, 'each one of which is institutionalized and expresses specific forms of social relationship and the corresponding social behaviour and social actions. For instance, the fact of living in a village, small town or a city produces distinctive groupings of people with the corresponding display of social relationships, behaviour and actions. The English distinction of county and country, the Indian distinciton of being a villager, a mofussil-man, or a city-dweller attests to this role of a demographic institution.

An institution will express the social relationships, behaviour and actions in a particular manner while there is commonality in them for a set of analogous (parallel) or homologous (originally common) institutions. The village panchayat, the town municipality and the city corporation represent a set of institutions for local self-government in India and give rise to a common set of relationships, behaviour and actions with reference to this form of consolidation of people. However, the customary rather than the contractual aspect of the relationships, behaviour and actions is clearly noticeable for the village panchayat, to a certain extent for the town municipalty, and the least for the city corporations.

We similarly find that the intellectual or the cultural activities of the people are manifest through various kinds of groupings, each of which displays a particular brand of social relationships, behaviour and actions while there is a commonality among them for these groupings. At one extreme, with respect to the establishments for formal learning and culture, there are the teacher-student, among students, among academics, and similarly structured relationships, and the corresponding kinds of social behaviour and sets of social actions. At the other extreme there are the least structured but the same forms of relationships, behaviour and actions in the regular but informal settings, as in the case of the Bengali middle class institution of *adda*, or even at a tea-shop, a street corner assembly, etc.

Thus, all meaningfully repetitive and sustained interactions of individuals emanate from the determined efforts and achievements of the people to consolidate their life process. These efforts and achievements are manifest by means of distinctive channels—the institutions—which regulate their course of behaviour and actions with reference to specific points depicting precise social relationships.

Over time, the institutions change in their form and content, and some of them may disappear. The economic content of the institution of family may produce more than one household (i.e., co-resident and commensal unities of persons): one in the ancestral village and the other in an urban settlement, as is not infrequently found in the Third World. On the other hand, the household with kin members and others may emerge as an institution for the promotion of rudimentary capitalist enterprises, as was found in Europe at the beginning of the capitalist era and is still noticeable in those places where the capitalist system of production has deeply penetrated into the peasant economy (e.g., in south Italy in Calabria and in Sicily).

The institution of caste may disappear from Indian society, which has also been predicted for the institution of state in the future perspective of world society. Religion has lost its secular function in Europe and, consequently, the social relationships, behaviour and actions the institution had enforced in the Middle Ages. On the other hand, religion has resumed its secular function in contemporary Israel, Iran and Pakistan, and has thus led to the emergence of new forms of social relationships, behaviour and actions.

The institution of *ashrama*, according to which the learner lived and worked in the *guru's* family and, in turn, was taught and maintained by him, is lost to India. With this has disappeared the specific form of teacher-student relationship and the corresponding behaviour patterns and actions. Also, the teacher-student relationship virtually anywhere in the world is no more the same as it was up to the first half of the present century and resembled the parent-child relationships: it is becoming contractual as one pays fees and receives education in return.

'Classes' in the Marxist schema have changed their form and content with the disappearance of the institution of feudalism, and may eventually be abolished from world society. The political institutions of India have undergone marked changes since the withdrawal of the British, and many erstwhile rebels have become stalwarts of the Establishment. Its effect on their changed social relationships, behaviour and actions vis-à-vis the people is only too apparent. On the other side, new sets of rebels have emerged on the social scene, along with their specific institutional affiliations and the corresponding forms of social relationships, behaviour, actions within and across the sets of rebels and with the masses.

However, the variations within and between a set of social institutions are governed by one or more relevant institution, just as the disappearance of one institution is governed by other institutions. As regards the smallest grouping in society, we find that any shift in the institutional role of the family to look after the young and the old must be commensurate with the appearance and proper functioning of the institutions for child care (e.g., creches) and for the senior citizens (e.g., old-age homes). The family as an institution may also be conceived to disappear, but only when its functions are delegated to another institution (e.g., the state in the schema of Aldous Huxley's *Brave New World*).

With regard to what is possibly the largest grouping in world society, we find that, on the formal political plane, feudal society was replaced by bourgeois society and the latter is governed by the newly emerged institution of parliamentarism. Moreover, contemporary bourgeois societies vary on this formal political plane according to the character of parliamentarism, with which monarchy too may be associated as in the UK, Sweden and the Netherlands. Further, bourgeois society is expected to be replaced by socialist society by means of the institutions of the socialist and the communist parties.

Thus, in order that society may exist and operate, a constellation of social institutions is always present to provide the mechanism to establish stable social relationships and the corresponding social behaviour and social actions. The institutions also provide the base and the spearhead for ushering in changes in society, leading to social transformation. Therefore, in the conceptual frame of reference for understanding society, social institutions occupy the fourth tier in the sequence of social action, social behaviour and social relationship.

However, the social institutions are neither observable nor deducible. They are also not interpretative. This point should be illustrated with reference to the agencies cited as institutions. Thus, a marriage seems to be observable but what is observed is a particular set of rites and rituals in the case of a sacred marriage, a set of civil procedures in the case of a secular marriage, and none of these or any other 'socially' sanctioned activity in the case of a companiate marriage. Yet, the institution of marriage is behind the observable interactions that are displayed by the regulation of privileges and obligations of sexual union in society.

Perhaps one might claim more confidently that kinship is observable because one can trace one's kin and affines in a genealogical chart. But any kinship network is made up of deducible kinship behaviour and interpretative kinship relations. Moreover, the kinship networks do not represent kinship as an institution: they constitute the structure by means of which the agency operates, as in the parallel instance of marriage of one form or the other.

The family, it will be argued, is not observable; but, at the same time, it may be claimed to be deducible in terms of its definition. The definition of a family, however, varies with respect to the stipulated objective attributes like co-residence, commensality and ownership of property, and the range of variability is widened in case the subjective attribute of who considers (himself or herself) to belong to which family is taken into account. Moreover, as for marriage and kinship networks, any set of families merely constitutes the structure by means of which the family as an institution operates.

The same set of conditions applies to any other institution already cited or which we may cite additionally. In sum, all phenomena in society have their respective sets of rites, rituals and procedures. Their definitions vary on objective and/or subjective grounds, as attested to by the perennial polemics in social science literature on their account. Therefore, what we observe or deduce about them does not automatically represent the institutions to which they refer.

Furthermore, the operative agencies behind all phenomena in society are not interpretative, because interpretation means expounding the meaning of a word, explaining or understanding a phenomenon in a specified manner. Social relationships, thus, interpret the meanings of the deduced social behaviour among groups of persons. But that *meaning* is not applicable to institutions, nor to their explanation; for that meaning is not yet conceived in a specified manner.

Therefore, social institution should be regarded as a *concept*, i.e., a 'general notion', an 'idea of class of objects' applied to social phenomena. This means that an institution has to be formed in the mind as representing the mechanics of a distinctive multitude of social actions, corresponding social behaviour, and the consequent social relationships. Thus determined subjectively, the concept of an institution may vary, as attested to by the concern of social science with defining the 'institutions': for instance, what exactly are the institutions of marriage, family, kinship, caste, religion, education, culture, capitalism, imperialism, nationalism?

However, science *abstracts* knowledge of the manifest and the latent, and, thus, of the immanent reality at the existing state of our information on the phenomenon concerned. This is how the 'body of knowledge' is organized and made evermore precise, unequivocal and comprehensive as we systematically accumulate and consolidate information on the phenomena. Chapter 2 discusses how sciencing society may become unequivocal and efficient. In that context, and in the light of the foregoing discussion, we should note here that a social institution as a concept should be regarded as a matter of *inference* to be drawn from the relevant multitude of social actions (which are observable), the corresponding social behaviour (which is deducible), and the consequent social relationships (which are interpretative).

Thus inferred, social institution occupies the pivotal position in the frame of reference developed for understanding society. This point will be discussed at the end of this chapter.

Social Group

The institutions operate through collectivites of individuals who are consolidated into 'social groups'. The groups are, therefore, formed in many ways in accordance with the institution(s) which produce one or the other kind of grouping.

Sexual partners are grouped by marriage. The grouping, however, can be of respective sets of a man and a woman in the case of monogamy or companiate marriage, of a man and several women in the case of a polygynous marriage, of several men and a woman in the case of a polyandrous marriage, and of several men and several women in the case of (i) the hypothetical group marriage, (ii) the 'composite' marriage reflecting both polygyny and polyandry, or (iii) the 'community living' practised by the 'angry young persons' in West Germany and elsewhere in the 1960s.

The institution of family forms kin groups which, according to the relational characteristics of the family members, may be of many kinds: nuclear, patrilineal-patrivirilocal, matrilineal-matriutrolocal, natolocal, avuncolocal, etc.

The institution of kinship leads to various kinds of groupings of sets of blood relatives (kin) and relatives by marriage (affines). Besides the family constituted of individuals related as kin and affines, there are the lineage groups (such as *kula* in Hindu society) which comprise kin related to an individual from the paternal *or* the maternal side. There are other kinds of lineage and filiation groupings while the clan (*gotra*) in Hindu society refers to all blood relatives descended from a mythical ancestor. The affinal groups also may be of many kinds, such as *kutumba* (in Hindu society), which comprises all those related to one another by his/her own marriage or that of the blood relatives. Similarly, the agnatic-affinal groups are formed in many ways: for instance, in Hindu society, one comprising those who are entitled to offer oblation to an ancestor (*sapinda*) and thus hold potential rights to the ancestor's property, another comprising those who form a distinctive genealogical tree (*vamsa*). The latter may be contemporarily equated with a 'family' in a configuration of human society or in the world at large; for instance, the mythical *yaduvamsa* and the non-mythical Birla family.

Thus engineered by an institution or the interplay of several institutions, larger and larger clusters of individuals are identified as social groups in terms of caste, religion, ethnicity, nationality, nation-state affiliation, social class formation in the Weberian sense, class formation in the Marxist sense, and so on. All these groups are identifiable in any one configuration of world society or for the world at large. Either way, the groups are in existence at a point in time and disappear or emerge over a period in time. This happens because people continually make efforts to sustain what they have achieved in life and to attain in future what they aspire for.

Spontaneously, therefore, society appears to us as a variable entity in terms of group formation of individuals. This point was illustrated at the beginning of this chapter and, therefore, the minimax definition of society was proposed: minimally, society is a group constituted of more than one person; and, maximally, of all human beings. However, out of the cauldron containing all individuals in society, any one of them is a constituent of multifarious collectivities (i.e., social groups), as he/she is subject to, and/or a supporter of, various social institutions. Therefore, while society is constituted of individuals by the fact of their entrance into collectivities, the contextual roles of the individuals and the groups they form are of no less importance in understanding society than the identification of the social groups.

This means that directly identifiable as they are, by themselves alone the social groups do not lead us to an understanding of 'what is society'. We are, thus, repeating the point we had made at the beginning of this chapter, but we may now add to it the following: While the minimax definition of society is *valid* in terms of forming social groups, the groups acquire *relevance* for an understanding of society with reference to their causal antecedents of social institutions and their operation with respect to apposite sets of social actions, behaviour and relationships.

This is why we have conceived of repetitive and meaningful interactions in terms of group-wise and not just individual-oriented actions and reactions. Social actions and social behaviour have been conceived, likewise, in terms of group formations which are expressed by means of social relationships. All this means is that (*i*) society cannot be understood without taking note of the matrix of variation (the mould) through which it operates, and (*ii*) the mould cannot be appreciated without the conceptual frame prepared for that purpose.

Apropos, the social groups should be regarded to compose the fifth and the final tier of the conceptual frame.

The Mould

It should be clear from the foregoing discussion that any segmental description of 'what is society' will be as fallacious as the Indian fable of seven blind men describing an elephant. One of them touched a leg and described the animal as the trunk of a tree, another touched the tail and described it as a rope, the third touched an ear and described the elephant as a winnowing fan, and so on. Similarly, to describe society as, respectively, a network of interactions, the structure of social action, the field of social behaviour, the web of social relationships, the interlocking of social institutions, or the congruence of social groups, would all be partially valid but incomplete in totality. We have, therefore, prepared the conceptual frame which *systemizes* these aspects in a hierarchical order for understanding 'what is society' by means of the process of 'how does society operate'.

However, the frame of reference cannot be conceived in a bi-dimensional plan of the five enumerated tiers, which one may be tempted to do for purposes of simplification. The social actions, behaviour and relationships are, of course, on one plane of two dimensions because they follow sequentially and in one direction. A set of homologous social actions is depicted as one particular social behaviour and, thus, the analogous sets of social actions form analogous sets of social behaviour. A set of social behaviour, in the sequence, denotes a particular social relationship, and thus the sets of behaviour patterns denote series of dyadic relations. Ultimately, by expressing group relations people are identified as belonging to one or the other social group because the same person must belong to many social groups. From action to group consolidation, the frame of reference for understanding society may, therefore, be conceived as on one plane of two dimensions.

In this manner we may conceive of *what* are the roles played by individuals in society. Therefore, society is also characterised as depicting a network of roles played by its constituents in group formation. However, the bi-dimensional frame to answer this *what* question does not elucidate *how* the roles are displayed. For this purpose, we are required to consider the tier depicting the social institutions, but that tier draws our attention to another dimension of the frame of reference because the social relationships emanate from one or the other social institution while the institutions operate by means of sets of social groups.

Therefore, on one plane there is a two-dimensional sequence between social relationships and institutions, on another the sequence between social institutions and social groups, and on a third plane the sequence between social relationships and social groups. The three planes in the frame of reference may be so arranged that while the social institutions are conceptually located on a different plane, they serve as the *link* between social relationships and social groups. As a result, the frame of reference should be of three, and not two, dimensions.

This manner of conceptualization of the frame of reference is of crucial importance to appreciate the statics and dynamics of society as a variable entity. For, by serving as the medium to express social relationships on the one side, and group formation on the other, the social institutions do not appear on the foreground of social actions, behaviour patterns, social relationships and social group consolidation. The institutions operate behind the social scene as the reservoir of multidirectional forces which, at a balance, hold society at equilibrium at a point in time and which, because of their unequal magnitude, change society over a period of time.

The three-dimensional frame of reference for understanding *how* society operates is shown in Figure 5. On the basis of this we can also conceive *what* is society, namely:

1. It is not a *random* assortment of individuals interacting in terms of personalized interactions.
2. It is not *exclusively* a network of social actions, or of social behaviour, or of social relationships, or of social institutions, or of social groups.

3. *Unilateral* stress on any one of these landmarks to conceptualize society would be fragmentary and fallacious.
4. The five landmarks are so related *systemically* that one cannot do without the other while each has a distinctive role to play in holding society and changing it.
5. Therefore, in order to appraise the five landmarks, we should bear in mind their respective characteristics with reference to the place, time and object (people) dimensions of variation in world society.

It follows from this that in order to understand society we should orient ourselves to the following course of reasoning which is incorporated in Figure 5.

1. While personal interactions are spontaneously observable, social action is a matter of *sustained observation* (or enumeration in the context of what is past).
2. Social behaviour, on the other hand, is a matter of *deduction*.
3. Social relationship, in the sequence of action and behaviour, is a matter of *interpretation*.
4. Social institution, in this context, is a matter of *inference*.
5. Lastly, social group is a matter of *identification* with respect to its causal antecedents of institutions on the one hand, and with reference to the operative principles of actions, behaviour and relationships on the other.

To sum up the discussion in this chapter, society should be conceived as a complex whole of individuals who are systematically integrated in various ways in terms of their

FIGURE 5

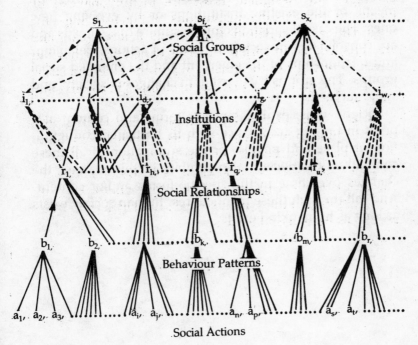

Frame of Reference

actions, behaviour and relationships. This whole is organized by the people for purposes of their existence and realization of their aspirations in life. These purposes have led in the past, and will lead in future, to the emergence of motivating agencies of social institutions which not only consolidate the individuals within a system of material and immaterial things but also impart to them a character beyond individuality.

Therefore, society is an entity which conditions the lives of people while allowing for undesigned individual variations within the limits of *casualness*. If, however, the individual variations are designed, these are institutionalized by means of the existing institutions or by evolving new ones. The casual variations thus assume a *causal* nexus and are consolidated in society in terms of actions, behaviour and relationships of the emergent and the emerged social groups. The groups try to usher in changes in society, and some succeed.

Society, thus, exhibits specific forms and content at a point in time in accordance with its particular configuration of place and people, or the summation of all these configurations. Society also exhibits in this manner the changes over time in the specific forms and/or content. And, all through these manoeuvres, human society exists as long as humankind exists.

2. SOCIOLOGY AND SOCIAL SCIENCE

The Issue

In Chapter 1 we have briefly discussed what it is that holds society as an entity at a point in time and how it is that society changes as a dynamic concern over time. In this context of understanding society, and briefly as before, we should examine the role of sociology in the realm of social science. This is necessary because the task of sociology is to understand and appraise society, but we notice from this perspective that unsystematic distinctions are not infrequently drawn between sociology and the other social science disciplines. For example, the task seems to devolve upon anthropology, psychology, political science and economics.

We also notice that these distinctions, made by the reflective minds of scholars, are sometimes superposed or superseded and, thus, obliterated by some other scholars. We speak, in that event, of economic sociology, social anthropology, social psychology, political sociology, and so on. Moreover, we sometimes label ourselves as sociologists and sometimes as anthropologists. Furthermore, we commonly combine subject matters, for instance, socio-economic, psycho-social, socio-political.

Thus, the relation between sociology and the other social science subjects emerges before us as an imprecise issue. The relation should undoubtedly be made precise in the context of understanding society. With this aim in view, we may begin by formulating the problem of treating sociology and other social science subjects as distinctive disciplines or as specializations emerging from a common base, i.e., a unitary social science discipline in place of unified social science disciplines.

The Problem

The term sociology stands for the 'science of society', which is also the meaning conveyed by the term 'social science'. More commonly, we speak of the 'social sciences', which further complicates our understanding of the matter involved; it is as if society is not a unitary but a unified expression of reality. Under the circumstances, we should agree to one of two formulations for sciencing society, bearing in mind that sciencing denotes a systematic and systemic exploration of causality of a facet of reality which, in the present instance, is the social reality. The formulations are as follows:

1. There are different bodies of knowledge which are organized as different disciplines, i.e., as distinctive branches of instructions on, and understanding and appraisal of, society.

2. There is one organized body of knowledge for the understanding and appraisal of society and, therefore, one discipline. Accordingly, the different aspects of society are examined by means of *specializations* in that discipline.

The two formulations may seem to be quibbling. One may ask: How does it matter whether we regard subjects like sociology, social anthropology, psychology, political science and economics as different social science disciplines or as specializations within the realm of social science? The answer in the present context would be that it matters because we should not be equivocal about the *generic* and the *specific* roles of sociology to understand and appraise society. This point deserves elucidation.

Sociology as a discipline by itself would. convey the sense that the distinctions among the social science subjects are of crucial importance while their interrelations are auxiliary, i.e., *helpful* toward a comprehensive understanding and appraisal of society. Sociology as a specialization in the discipline of social science would denote just the opposite conditions: (*i*) the interrelations among the social science subjects are of crucial importance in understanding and appraising society comprehensively, and (*ii*) the distinctions among these subjects are of auxiliary relevance to a more and more precise rendering of our understanding and appraisal of society.

Thus, according to the first formulation, we conceive sociology as *analogous* (parallel) to economics, psychology, etc., in the universe of social science disciplines. According to the second, sociology and all such subjects as are concerned with the understanding and appraisal of society are conceived to be *homologous* (common in origin) within the discipline of social science. We should bear in mind that the possibility of drawing a relation between sociology and social science in either of these two ways may not be discounted. However, between the two, we should ascertain the more efficient manner of distinguishing and interrelating the social science subjects, and in particular reference to sociology; for, it is only in this way that we should be able to appreciate unequivocally the role of sociology in understanding and appraising society.

Because we do not usually attend to this issue, or even pose it as a problem, our appreciation of the subject matter of sociology remains rather amorphous. Sometimes we regard sociology as an *omnibus* and sometimes as a *residual* subject in the universe of social science. The omnibus criterion is attested to by the fact that the textbooks and handbooks of sociology incorporate something of economics, political science, demography, psychology, etc. At the same time, the residual criterion of sociology is testified by the fact that its thrust is on those topics which are not directly (or at all) incorporated under the above-mentioned subjects—for example, marriage, kinship, family, community organization and social stratification.

In the latter respect, anthropology and sociology tend to deal with the same subject matter. However, a distinction between these two subjects is virtually non-existent today. The same scholar identifies himself or herself as an anthropologist or a sociologist as and when the occasion arises. On the other hand, by accepting both the omnibus and the residual character of sociology, but in a formal sense only, we tend to avoid the issue of social science specializations or disciplines by employing hyphenated labels for the appraisal of social phenomena: for instance, socio-economic, socio-demographic, socio-political.

These attempts create the problem of *identification*, which is succeeded by the problem of *duplication*, and, in a logical sequence, lead to the problem of *conceptualization*, namely, what is sociology. We should therefore examine this sequence.

Any manifestation in society is broadly characterized as 'social', and sociology is generally regarded as dealing with that which is 'social'. This is how sociology acquires its omnibus meaning which is conveyed through labels like social anthropology, social philosophy, social biology and social history. The meanings of these terms would be precise or redundant in case we can unequivocally define what is 'social' and thus lead sociology to shed its omnibus character. This, therefore, has been the concern of social science in recent times and two terms have been coined in that context: *societal* and *social*. What is societal is easy to define—all that happens in society. Social, in that context, would refer to a particular segment of the societal; but, to date, what is social begs a precise definition. The upshot is that sociology remains as an omnibus or a residual subject in the realm of social science.

In its disciplinary orientation, sociology is usually regarded as a residual subject, i.e., its subject matter deals with those aspects of society which are not regarded to fall under apparently clear demarcations of respective branches of social science knowledge like economics, politics and psychology. The residual connotation, however, is essentially formal and raises the question of where to draw the limit in the formal arrangements of the subject matter for economics, politics, psychology, etc. It also raises the omnibus connotation of whether 'culture', 'ideology', 'ecology', 'demography', etc., should or should not fall within the purview of sociology *per se*.

There are divergent views on this question of limit which cannot be resolved unless and until we develop an unequivocal concept of what is social as distinct from all that is societal. And, so long as we do not develop this concept, the imprecise appreciation of the 'social' characteristics will create problems of identification and duplication of the subject matter of sociology.

For example, the occupation of a person has been standardized in the classification sponsored by the International Labour Office as the nature of job(s) performed by him or her in agriculture, handicraft production, machine industries, transport, communication, mining, and such other economic sectors of society. Occupation is, therefore, spontaneously reckoned as an 'economic' attribute. But, then, why are occupational hierarchy, mobility up or down the hierarchy, etc., considered within the purview of sociology in terms of social stratification and social mobility?

Similarly, does a co-resident and commensal kin group form a 'social' unit of the family as an institution or an 'economic' unit of consumption (and also of production in the 'peasant' societies) under the institution of household formation? Is class in the Marxist schema an economic, a political, or a social entity? Is social class in the Weberian schema an economic, a psychological, or a social entity? Should we consider 'youth revolt', a so-called 'tribal' movement, or an ethnic upsurge as a social and/or a political phenomenon?

Many more examples can be cited and it may be recalled that we often attempt to bypass this quandary by using hyphenated labels like socio-economic, psycho-social, or socio-political. But the problem of identification of what is 'social' remains, such as, where does the 'socio' compo-nent of the hyphenated terms end and the 'economic' or other component begin? Alternatively, should we con-sider the hyphenated terms to possess meanings of their own? In that case, do we not revert to the omnibus charac-terization of sociology from its popular residual character?

Contemporarily, there is another attempt to bypass the quandary by drawing attention to the particular nuance of the societal phenomena and not to the phenomena them-selves. For example, it is now well-established that the family is the medium of various kinds of manifestation in society which may be categorized as economic, demo-graphic, religious, 'social', etc. Similarly, 'youth revolt' may be the expression of, and may simultaneously release, sets of variation which may be categorized as political, cultural, psychological and 'social'. However, this attempt also does not resolve the problem, precisely because it lacks a conceptual framework. On the other hand, it transfers the problem of identification into a problem of duplication.

The problem of duplication is noticeable with respect to the subject matter for 'social research', whether or not the topics of research are categorized in detail in order to exhibit respective nuances of the phenomena concerned. For example, while we may appositely define family struc-tures according to the nature and the extent of kinship characteristics of their constituents, can we compartmen-tally study the sociology, psychology, economics and poli-tics of the family without cutting across one or the other aspect of this societal manifestation? Similarly, while the rural and the urban areas may be distinguished according to certain attributes of habitation, may we exclusively consider the topic of urbanization as a subject for social, demographic, economic, or socio-economic, socio-demo-graphic, economic-demographic research?

The problem is also seen in contemporary attempts by social science to overreach (not in a pejorative sense, of course) other scientific disciplines. Demography and ecology are fair examples in this context, as also social biology, social medicine, human geography, and so on.

The problem is clearly manifest with respect to the categorization of societal phenomena and their nuances under different headings in the national and international handbooks of statistics. We should take particular note of duplication in this context because, as precisely formulated by the renowned statistician R.A. Fisher (1946:1), statistics refer to the (*i*) population, (*ii*) variation, and (*iii*) methods of reduction of the data with reference to a phenomenon or a set of phenomena. 'Social' or any other kind of statistics, therefore, is first concerned with an unequivocal demarcation of the respective populations which are to be considered as 'social' or any other, be it with reference to the phenomena *en bloc* or the nuances they register.

The statistical classification of the subjects pertaining to social science is, therefore, an important pointer to the confusion which prevails because of their *formal* arrangements. We should not ignore the issue faced in this context by assuming that the confusion is caused by the statisticians who may not be experts in social science. We should bear in mind that leading social scientists were involved in evolving these classifications by UN agencies and others.

Therefore, it is useful for us to note that the size, structure and distribution of population, births and deaths, migration, etc., are categorized as 'demographic' and 'social' statistics. Health, sanitation, nutrition, etc., are labelled 'medical' and 'social'. Employment, labour conditions, income and expenditure, etc., fall under the categories of 'economic', 'social', and so on. Social welfare and security appear to be entirely 'social', but there is also the label of 'welfare economics'. Similarly, crime and justice fall under the categories of judicial, psychological, and social statistics.

The succession of the problems of identification and duplication, thus, leads us to the basic problem of conceptualization. With the accumulation of social science knowledge and the ever-growing complexities in society, it has become hazardous to distinctly conceive of a phenomenon as 'social' or 'economic', even though the distinction appears to be clearly drawn. Moreover, the hazards are not removed by focusing our attention on the sortable nuances of the phenomenon. In this context, education serves us with an appropriate example.

Education is universally regarded as a 'social' phenomenon because its objective is the advancement of learning in society. However, the establishment of educational institutions and facilities is also an 'economic' enterprise to the entrepreneurs in many nation-states, and this may not be less profitable than establishing a small-scale manufacturing industry. Appositely, while an educational establishment advances one form of learning in society, a manufacturing establishment does another by means of various kinds of social relationships which are complementary among the large number of comrades at work and contradictory in terms of the bosses and the underlings. In intensity, coverage and quality, this form of learning would be absent in an agricultural community: a point which promotes the consideration of industrialization as not merely an 'economic' but also a 'social' and 'psychological' phenomenon.

One may be accused of ridiculing the sanctity of education by linking it with mundane matters like the manufacture of goods instead of learned persons. Let us therefore recall the topic of urbanization. Given the definition of an urban area, urbanization seems to be a matter of density of population, virtual absence of agricultural production, and the municipal organization of the constituent population. Therefore, the phenomenon appears to be purely 'demographic'. We should ask ourselves, accordingly: what is 'social' about urbanization, as the process is frequently characterized, unless (*i*) everything that happens in society is regarded to be social, or (*ii*) the term is meant to refer to certain *distinct but common* characteristics of all societal phenomena?

The first alternative forecloses any discussion on what is social by removing the distinction between the concepts of societal and social. But the distinction is obviously useful for the comprehension of social reality in terms of its various manifestations. Therefore, from the 1960s in particular, social scientists have attempted to establish a link among the social science subjects in terms of *behaviourism*. The Behavioural School has gained prominence, especially with those who tend to subscribe to the basic approach of Max Weber (and like-minded social scientists) toward the appraisal of social reality.

However, for the present we should recall our discussion in Chapter 1 that social behaviour can subsume social action but cannot anticipate the institutional distinctions and correlations with reference to social relationships on the one hand and the social groups on the other. We may recall the example cited of a person touching the feet of elders and a shoe-shine boy doing the same vis-à-vis a client. This is a pointer to the fact that exclusively on the plane of behaviourism, the causality and predictability of societal phenomena would be a matter of assumption, conjecture and speculation. As we shall later discuss in some detail, sciencing society will not then be based on *probabilistic inferences* to be drawn from a rigorous analysis of society in being and becoming.

Even so, the Behavioural School is a more articulate attempt to appraise social reality than what was attempted before, although it fails to render a precise, unequivocal and comprehensive understanding of society. However, while it serves as a more effective method to bypass the dilemma of societal and social than the conjugation of social science 'disciplines' by hyphenated terms, one cannot really pass the issue by.

Therefore, in order to appreciate the distinctions and interrelations between sociology and the other specializations (the 'disciplines') in social science, we must come to an unequivocal understanding of the *functional difference* between the formulations societal and social in place of drawing all sorts of formal distinctions or avoiding the issue. For this it is necessary to examine the historical and contemporary developments in the realm of social science because that would provide the *content* to the nature of the problem with which we are dealing.

The Nature of the Problem

From the time sciencing society was submerged in humanistic studies the substantive universe of social science has been continually enriched with the formulation and reformulation of new subjects for study. This is evident from the successively enlarged social science curricula of universities, especially in the second half of the present century. Political science is now clearly separated from economics on the one hand and from government or politics on the other. Cultural anthropology was distinguished from social anthropology in the 1920s and the 1930s, but the two have assumed a coexistence and an equation since the 1940s. Social psychology, however, is clearly distinguished from clinical psychology. History is reckoned as a social science subject, and others, like public administration, demography and ecology, have established their separate claims within the domain of social science.

All these subjects, as also those which have retained their nomenclature all along (e.g., economics and sociology) are continually accumulating new matter for study and research. This is attested to by the syllabi for their study in the universities, and the journals which are brought out on their respective fields of specialization. It follows that the subjects require specialized instruction and, therefore, these are usually specified as different disciplines.

Thus, for a while distinctions among 'disciplines' became the keynote of social science. The distinctions were cultivated to such an extent that the appraisal of reality with reference to the same configuration of society, or even the same societal phenomenon, became virtually unintelligible for all except the specialists of one discipline. For instance, this holds true with reference to the 'village studies' and the 'peasant studies' in India, conducted by different brands of social scientists in the second half of the present century. Previously, social anthropologists, sociologists, political scientists and economists had a common orientation to these studies; but, from the 1950s in particular, their approaches became more and more divergent. Our first formulation that the social science disciplines are analogous (parallel) was thus enforced.

Needless to say, one aspect of growth is specialization. It is obvious, therefore, that the social science subjects must become more and more specialized as knowledge accumulates. However, the growth must not be cancerous as this would destroy the understanding and appraisal of society as an entity. Social scientists are not oblivious to this danger and, therefore, reacted when they felt that specialization *ad nauseum* may lead to arid abstractions and thus jeopardize a comprehensive appraisal of social reality.

Somewhat later in the Third World than in the First and the Second Worlds, the need for undertaking interdisciplinary studies was therefore emphasized by social scientists. The Behavioural School provided the platform for this venture. Doubts were thus mooted against the first formulation of mutually exclusive social science disciplines, despite the fact that interdisciplinary orientation does not reject the characterization of social science subjects as analogous disciplines.

The matter went beyond doubt, and a new approach toward the appraisal of social reality was indicated. Radhakamal Mukerjee, one of the pioneers in Indian sociology, posited the view that what is required for a precise and comprehensive appraisal of social reality is not an interdisciplinary but a *transdisciplinary* orientation. In this proposal, which he made during his Presidential Address to the Third All-India Sociological Conference in 1957 (Mukerjee 1961), we find support for our second formulation that the social science subjects are homologous in character. This point was also implied by another pioneer in Indian sociology, D.P. Mukerji, at his Presidential Address to the First All-India Sociological Conference in 1955.

Perhaps, even now, the two pioneers will not find support to their viewpoint from the general run of social scientists. However, we should bear in mind that they did not undermine the need for specialization in respective social science subjects. But, along with specialization, they underlined the need to integrate all social science subjects on a common base. Thus, D.P. Mukerji (1958) stated the role of sociology vis-à-vis other social science subjects at the Conference in 1955 in the following manner:

Sociology has a floor and a ceiling, like any other social science, but its speciality consists in its floor

being the ground-floor of all types of social disciplines, and its ceiling remaining open to the sky. Neglect of the social base often leads to arid abstractions,
as in recent economics. On the other hand, much of
empirical research in anthropology and in psychology has been rendered futile because its fields have
so far been kept covered. Yet, within this mansion of
sociology the different social disciplines live. Insofar
as they live on the same floor, they are bound to come
into conflict with each other in the name of autonomy.
To pursue the analogy, they seek to divide the house
into flats and close the door against each other. But a
stage comes when exclusiveness ceases to pay for the
living. Such a stage seems to have been reached by
nearly all the social sciences.

The point made by D.P. Mukerji is seen to have been
conceptually and operationally enforced by all social science 'disciplines', although its implication often passes
our notice. Therefore, let us briefly examine the core
issues in different social science subjects.

Economics today is a highly specialized subject, but it is
moving away from the viewpoint that it deals with the
relation *of* human beings with the material goods and services in terms of what is idealized as 'rational' behaviour.
More and more, economics is now regarded as the study
of the relation *among* human beings with respect to material goods and services and on the variable axis of 'social
behaviour'. The controversy in this respect, as between
Robbins (1932) and Sweezy (1946) on the nature and significance of economic science, is now dated. This shows
that while economics specializes in the material goods and
services, it draws *commonality* with other social science
subjects with respect to ever-accumulating information and
analysis of the social actions, behaviour, relationships,

institutions and group formation in human life. It means that, to be useful for society and the people, economics is less and less engrossed in arid abstractions in terms of any idealized and deterministic concept of 'rational' behaviour of humankind. Explicitly or not, the subject is thus treated as having a common origin (i.e., as homologous and not analogous) with other social science subjects.

Similarly, by tracing its antecedents to politics and government, political science was, at a time, deeply concerned with the manoeuvres of centralized power blocs or *real-politik*. For these manoeuvres one society or various configurations of world society merely provided the field of operation and the people were treated as pawns in the game. More and more, however, political science takes an analytic and a comprehensive view of society and the constituent people, as does economics today, in respect of its particular area of specialization. Current studies and research in political science testifies to this change in focus. It is now concerned with such topics as the building of a nation-state or the plasticity of nation and state formation; North-South, South-South and East-West dialogues; dependency or mutual aid of the nation-states; 'social' movements and politicization of the people; and so on.

Studies and research in psychology have moved beyond individuals and attained a societal character. Matters of mind are not given a 'social' connotation purely on the basis of theories evolved from clinical experience or laboratory findings on individuals. The change is underlined by the psychologists' interest in analyzing 'communal' tension, 'social' pathology, etc. Their specialization in industrial psychology and even 'village studies' testifies to the same, as also their participation with other brands of social scientists in ascertaining the quality of life desired by the people in terms of perceptual and behavioural variables.

Likewise, demography is no more confined to the perimeter previously prescribed by the actuaries. Its societal character is now manifest in the details of the topics for study and research in reference to the growth, decay and movement of population. Concurrently, specialization in its subject matter has brought forth labels like 'economic demography'.

We notice the same course of specialization and integration of the social science 'disciplines' with respect to those subjects for study and research which did not claim any discipline-wise categorization in social science. For example, religion was the prerogative of the theologists and, later, some social anthropologists and sociologists became interested in the subject. But, for some decades now, economists, political scientists and psychologists are no less concerned with the subject.

Then there is the case of history as a 'discipline' under humanities. While specialization in the economic, political and social (= cultural) aspects of the chronology of events over time has gone on for quite some time, over the last few decades it is being increasingly regarded as a 'social science' discipline. Moreover, in recent years, new specializations have emerged on the one hand (e.g., contemporary history, ethnohistory) and, on the other, the subject is treated as providing the time dimension for study and research in all social science subjects.

The dual course of specialization and integration of all social science subjects, which is obvious today, points to the eventual redundancy of some subjects which for a long time were identified as distinctive disciplines. Social anthropology is an interesting case in this context. It has flourished in Europe and North America, and was imported with strong support from the rulers in the colonies. With the demise of the Empire from the middle of the present century, it is losing its ground as a distinctive 'discipline'.

In many universities it has become a specialization in one or the other social science 'discipline', while its persistence as a discipline in other universities is without much vigour. Furthermore, its fresh appearance as a discipline in any university has hardly been noticed in recent years.

These developments in the realm of social science serve as a pointer to examine the *links* among the social science subjects with respect to their specialization and integration at the same time, which may also reduce or nullify the need for one such subject to be considered exclusively and disparately. These links should indicate the functional distinctions and the interrelations between the formulations of societal and social and, thus, suggest the solution to the problem we have posed regarding what is sociology with reference to social science.

Toward a Solution

It should be clear from the foregoing discussion that the social science subjects emerged in the kingdom of knowledge with reference to particular societal contexts. At that point, therefore, they could be reckoned as distinctive bodies of knowledge or separate disciplines. But, with the continual accumulation of knowledge with reference to the place, time and people dimensions of variation in human society, the maintenance of disciplinary boundaries has proved to be inadequate today with respect to all social science subjects. What has actually happened is that the contexts to viewing these subjects have changed, and the revised contexts of higher orders have transformed the social science disciplines into specializations within the unitary discipline of social science.

Thus, so long as the context to economics as a branch of

knowledge was confined to the relation *of* humans with material goods and services, it could be regarded as a distinctive discipline. But today we view economics in the context of relations *among* humans with respect to the material goods and services. Against this revised context to explicate economics, its disciplinary boundary becomes hazy and is virtually lost. From the beginning of its expertise, it interacts with the other branches of knowledge on human society and, thus, it turns into a specialization in the realm of social science in the perspective of understanding and appraising society.

Similarly, so long as politics was almost exclusively concerned with *realpolitik* (i.e., the deliberations and manoeuvres of the statesman on how to seize and hold power and adjust its relation among different states), it could be considered as a separate social science discipline with a distinct context. But if, as today, power is also viewed with respect to the people, their leaders, and the power blocs they thus form in a nation-state or in the world at large, the context to political science is raised to a higher order. As a result, government or politics ceases to be a distinctive discipline. In its place, political science emerges as a specialization in the context of social science as the distinctive discipline which deals with a body of knowledge for understanding and appraising society.

This kind of transformation is obvious in the contexts of clinical and social psychology, demography in its early phase and today, ecology and social ecology, biology and social biology, medicine and social medicine, and so on. The case of sociology and its twin anthropology is not dissimilar.

As long as the understanding and appraisal of social reality were the prerogatives of the social philosophers, the context to the subject matter of sociology with reference to the 'civilized' societies (*civitus*, according to L. H. Morgan

[1964]) and of anthropology with reference to the 'primitive' societies (*societus*, according to L. H. Morgan [1964]) was simple and exclusive to other social science disciplines. It was concerned with those aspects of people's lives and living which are essential to hold society as an entity but are regarded as of a residual nature to the topics dealt with by disciplines like economics, politics and psychology. Therefore, the primary terms of reference to sociology and anthropology have been regarded as the institutions of marriage, family, kinship, status and prestige ranking of social groups, community organization, etc., and, ultimately, the social structure.

But beyond this kind of disciplinary orientation of sociology (and of its twin anthropology), it possesses a generic meaning today in the light of the distinction drawn between the societal and the social. The societal concept could attribute a disciplinary distinction to the social science subjects so long as a comprehensive understanding and appraisal of society was beyond the terms of reference to social science. But, once this (i.e., the appraisal of social reality) is considered the ultimate objective of social science, all its 'disciplines' turn into specializations with the connotation of being social in that context of a higher order.

At that state, sociology attains its generic meaning of treating society as a product and a process in the light of the societal operations described in Chapter 1. In other words, an integrative function devolves upon sociology to bring all social science subjects together and beyond an interdisciplinary stance which can artificially retain the disciplinary contexts of economics, politics, psychology, demography, ecology, sociology, etc. This is the meaning of a transdisciplinary approach to social science, for the operation of which sociology has a vital role to play in the course of raising the contexts to all social science disciplines on to a higher order and integrating them as specializations within the unitary discipline of social science.

Viewed in this manner, the variable contexts to the social science disciplines become the *classificatory* variables of the unitary discipline of social science because the discipline classes the variable contents of the same entity, namely, the society as a product and a process. It follows that the classificatory variables are integrated for an analytic-comprehensive understanding and appraisal of society, as also the contents (i.e., the subject matter or the *measure* variables) of all social science subjects.

This is increasingly how the relation between sociology and social science is viewed today—in practice, at any rate, if not also in theory. The attempt is particularly noticeable with respect to the schools of thought which have emerged in the last quarter of the twentieth century because of the inadequacy of the Behavioural School in unravelling social reality by introducing interdisciplinary research which keeps the 'disciplinary' boundaries intact.

However, in this introductory presentation of the relation between sociology and social science we need not discuss the above-mentioned cross-currents among the academics. Nonetheless, we may briefly introduce the procedure for treating in a unitary manner the contexts to social science 'disciplines' as classificatory variables of the discipline of social science. Also, in order that the ensuing relation between sociology and social science is precisely appreciated, we should examine the manner in which to treat the contents of the social science subjects, i.e., the measure variables.

Procedure

The concept of measurement seems to create a block in the thinking process of many social scientists, notably of sociologists and anthropologists. They claim to pursue 'human science' which, according to them, is not amenable to measurement of its contents. Economists and demographers will not accept this statement, nor will the majority of psychologists and political scientists. However, the basic fallacy of the debate lies in our common understanding of what is measurement, which is usually equated with quantification. Quantification, on the contrary, is the last stage of ascertaining the 'extent or quantity of (a thing) by comparison with fixed *unit* or with object of known size', which is the definition of measurement according to the Concise Oxford Dictionary.

According to this generally accepted definition, measurement proceeds from a *nominal* distinction drawn between *this* object as different from *that* object. For example, in contemporary India, the Muslims are permitted to be polygynous but monogamy is enforced for the Hindus.

Proceeding to the next step, measurement attains an *ordinal* distinction when one object is not only differentiated from another but is also rated as of a higher order of intensity or complexity. Thus, to pursue the above example, it may be found that although polygyny is permissible among Muslims, not many of them are polygynous, while some Hindus are surreptitiously polygynous.

Ordinal distinctions of this kind, as found among a set of things, may be *qualitatively* described as illustrated above, or, in the light of the increasing intensity or complexity that the set of objects depicts, they may be ordained *quantitatively*. For example, the unilineal joint family presents a higher order of complexity in kinship organization than a nuclear family, while a collateral joint family exhibits the same complexity of a still higher order and a bilateral joint family does the same of an even higher order. Therefore, these family types may be graduated as nuclear = 1, unilineal joint family = 2, collateral joint family = 3, and bilateral family = 4.

It will be noted that for quantitative-ordinal distinction any *equal* distance is not attributed between the numerals 1 and 2, 2 and 3, and 3 and 4 in the case of the above example. Thus, quantification would be complete when the things in a set can be so arranged that they form a series of 1, 2, 3, 4, ..., in which the consecutive numbers register a *unit-interval* distance, i.e., of 1 unit between the numerals 1 and 2, 1 unit between 2 and 3, 1 unit between 3 and 4, and so on. By adhering to the above example, this point may be illustrated, for instance, with respect to the kinship distances (by generational and collateral expansions) among the family members. In this case, a conjugal family without children (i.e., of husband and wife only) will be located at the zero point of the scale of quantification. However, in this introductory volume we need not discuss this complex procedure of measurement up to quantification.

What, on the other hand, needs to be emphasized is that measurement is *sui generis* to any set of observations or enumeration of objects, their analysis, and the comprehension of the subject matter they refer to. This is true for any empirical science—physical, biological and social. The point, then, is of the extent to which the nominal to the unit-interval scale of measurement has been (and can be) applied to a set of objects without affecting the intrinsic merit of the subject matter. Contrary to this standpoint, anti-measurers and anti-quantifiers were no less found among economists in the past as they are found today among anthropologists and sociologists.

However, with respect to the pursuit of sciencing, anti-measurement in social science is not the issue: it is a superstition carried on by an obscure metaphysical concept of 'human science'. The issue, on the one hand, is at what stage of measurement can a set of objects be realistically considered and, on the other, how the different contexts to social science subjects may, on that base, be treated as classificatory variables.

Because of its hangover, sociology (and anthropology) in the aforesaid context of a specific (= residual) subject in social science seldom deals with those objects to which the unit-interval scale of measurement has been applied. Nevertheless, from a nominal scale of measurement these objects are now frequently raised to the qualitative and, also, to the quantitative ordinal scale, as illustrated above. In economics, on the other hand, most of the objects it deals with are fully quantified, and the other social science subjects today fall between the range indicated by sociology (and anthropology) on the one side and economics on the other. Therefore, although not in its final form and content, a base for valid measure variables from all social science subjects is available today to link them with reference to their contexts, as found relevant, necessary and efficient for understanding and appraising society. The point is best clarified by examples.

Prior to 1957, polygynous marriage was equally permissible among Hindus and Muslims in India. In the first half of the nineteenth century, Pandit Iswar Chandra Vidyasagar vigorously collected mass support from the Hindus for the enactment of laws to (*i*) prohibit polygyny, and (*ii*) permit widow remarriage. He was successful with the second reform measure, although widow remarriage among the Hindus has yet to become a general phenomenon in society. On the other hand, he was unsuccessful regarding the first measure, but the incidence of polygyny had become rare in society long before the enactment against it. Why did this happen?

Several hypotheses have been put forward in this context, amongst which two are particularly worth noting:

(*i*) the steady economic deterioration of society as a whole does not permit one to maintain more than one wife and children, and (*ii*) modernization of society has changed the traditional outlook of the people toward polygynous marriage. Obviously, these two hypotheses refer to the contexts of economics and psychology against which the cultural (= sociological and anthropological) object of the incidence of polygynous marriage should be examined.

The economic context may be presented by classifying the marriageable males by their income or wealth treated as unit-interval items of information. Correspondingly, the psychological context may classify the same persons by their qualitative or quantitative ordinal attributes in the light of a schema of tradition to modernity. By thus transforming two social science contexts into classificatory variables, they may be juxtaposed, separately and jointly, against the measure variable of percentage incidence of polygynous to total marriages in a sample of several generations or with reference to the population census data for decades.

In this way we should be able to ascertain how, with reference to different strata of the social structure, the economic and the psychological contexts are respectively or jointly efficient for explaining the disappearance of polygyny before any legislation was enacted to prohibit it. For example, the economic context may be more appropriate to the impoverished people, and the psychological context to the relatively prosperous.

In the foregoing example the measure variable is concerned with the context of sociology (and anthropology) and the classificatory variable with the contexts of economics and psychology. We may next illustrate how these three contexts of the social science subjects may be combined as classificatory variables in order to present the social structure, and demography may provide the measure variable. A topical example is the number of children per couple, which is of crucial importance to the family planning programme in contemporary India.

Biologically, a man and a woman can produce many children during their fertile years, but in no society are the couples found to produce children *ad lib*. However, the propensity to produce many children was presumed by some sociologists and psychologists to be characteristic of Asian people in general and Indians in particular. The arguments put forward were: (*i*) cultural (= sociological), such as, the Hindus need sons to offer oblation to the departed ancestors, (*ii*) psychological, such as, the Muslims want sons to enhance family prestige, (*iii*) economic, such as, the prosperous but traditional families desire many children, and (*iv*) economic-cultural-psychological, such as, the prosperous but modern families desire one or two children or none at all. But all these contexts (emerging from various social science subjects) are seen from empirical studies to yield diverse measures of the demographic variable of the number of children per couple.

In Southeast Asia in general and in India in particular, the optimum number of children desired by a couple is seen to be three or four. The reason given by the majority is that an average couple cannot maintain a family larger than this. However, empirical studies in India have shown that this optimal number of three to four children varies widely according to social structural distinctions attributable to the sociological, the psychological, and the economic contexts. By the combination of these contexts, the social structural distinctions may be broadly placed under four distinctive categories.

1. At the bottom of the social hierarchy are placed the truly untouchables who eke out a living to somehow survive. They are the nightsoil-bearers, sweepers, earth-cutters, and sundry labourers of all kinds. For their survival, they

employ child labour and, therefore, produce as many children as possible subject to maintenance of their day to day living. In this case, it is economic scarcity (and not prosperity) that is found to register a high couple–children ratio.

2. Economic prosperity, however, stimulates the couple–children ratio for another stratum of the social structure. This stratum is composed of the wholesale merchants and specialized artisans (e.g., the workers on precious stones), who belong to the trading and artisan castes, and the landlords, who are in large measure upper caste Hindus. They need several sons to look after their business interests and their real estates and properties, and, as a result, produce large families.

3. But, economic prosperity in alliance with specific aspects of the sociological and psychological contexts may sharply reduce the couple–children ratio. This is exemplified by the thin stratum of highly educated, mostly caste-Hindu, upper middle class people living on very well paid jobs, like executives and managers of reputable firms. To this social stratum, the production of children is not a societal necessity for survival, security, or material prosperity; it is a matter of personal choice which, as modern elite, they exercise for having no children, one son or a daughter, or a son and daughter. They do not want many children because they would not then be able to rear them as befitting their social status while they are affluent enough not to regard sons as social security in old age.

4. Finally, there is the general mass of people who somehow manage an average middle class standard in both urban and rural India, while belonging to various castes and creeds. The couples representing this mass want, respectively, a son for security in old age, and another for insurance against any calamity that may befall the first

son. This psychology, sociology and economy of retaining their quality of life in old age, in lieu of adequate savings and investments, lead them toward a family of three to four children; for there is the equal chance that a child will be a son or a daughter.

We may cite other examples from empirical social research to illustrate the fact that the contexts of diverse social science subjects are converted into classificatory variables in order to measure their intrinsic characteristics in an intertwined manner. There is no doubt that contemporary social research is proceeding along this line, be it under the aegis of sociology (and anthropology), psychology, political science, demography, etc. This is substantiated by the articles published in those journals which ostensibly belong to these respective subjects.

Economics may seem to have charted an esoteric path for its own sake and thus have produced a number of technocrats. However, rooted in society, it cannot escape its context being transformed into classificatory variables of the unitary social science discipline. In the light of substantive writings on this subject, this is found to be as true for neoclassical economists as for the Marxist and all other intermediary brands of specialists in the subject of economics.

Thus it is that besides its residual-specific role sociology has attained today a generic-integrative role in the discipline of social science because, as explained in Chapter 1, it is concerned with the *totalities* of social action, social behaviour, social relationships, social institutions, and the social groups of today, in the past, and for the future. Therefore, the contexts for all social science subjects of specialization are finally integrated by the specialization of sociology assuming a generic character. From this perspective, the relation between sociology and social science draws our attention to the ultimate objective of sciencing society.

Sciencing Society

'Sciencing' is not yet a frequently used expression; however, it aptly captures the pursuit of knowledge in order to systematically comprehend a phenomenon by answering five sequential questions: What is it? How is it? Why is it? What will it be? What should it be? Phenomenon, in this context, refers to any thing, the properties of which are sufficiently known for its identification but not yet fully known for its adequate comprehension. Human society or any one of its configurations with reference to a place, a time and a people is thus a phenomenon. Therefore, the understanding of society depends on apposite answers to the first three questions of *what, how* and *why*; and its appraisal at present or in the future perspective depends on answering the last two questions of what *will* and what *should* society be.

The first question (what is it?) refers to an overall description of society; the second (how is it?) to a formal explanation of its operation *within* a system: a system defined as a complex whole which can be examined in the light of its mutually distinguished but interrelated components. At the beginning, all social science subjects, subject to their respective contexts, were engrossed with these two questions in order to describe and explain a society in terms of its structure and its function within a system.

So long as a system persists (and, on the whole, the social system must persist), these two descriptive and formally explanatory questions will not lose their relevance in understanding society. However, systematic changes do take place in human society, and some of these changes may acquire a *supra-systemic* character, i.e., the apposite changes are qualitatively different from the past and beyond fluctuations and oscillations within a given system.

The supra-systemic changes encounter situations where one system has been (or is at the point of being) replaced by another system. It is necessary to explain these changes for understanding the dynamics of society.

For example, it cannot be denied today that, historically, the primary classless societies were replaced by class societies, or capitalism as a system replaced feudalism. Such qualitative changes in society may be examined in other ways, as has been done by some pioneers in social science. But these variations need not be examined in this introductory volume, just as we need not examine the contemporary changes from capitalism to socialism or reversal to *status quo ante.*

However, the point that we must consider in this context is that society is always in a state of *dynamic equilibrium,* and not in a state of static or relative equilibrium or perpetual disequilibrium. It registers equilibrium as a product at a time point, and as a process it entails qualitative changes over a time period. Therefore, the phenomenon of society cannot be fully understood from any overall description of its organization and structure, and a formal explanation of its function within a particular system. Consequently, for a fuller understanding of society we raise the third question, why is it, with reference to supra-systemic changes in society. This necessary (and not only relevant) question bears the potential of a causal (and not just a formal) explanation of what has happened to a society and is happening today.

Sciencing society (i.e., a systematic understanding and appraisal of a phenomenon) cannot, therefore, make a true *beginning* without treating the three questions conjointly, namely, what, how, and why it is. We may illustrate this point by citing an example familiar to contemporary Indian sociologists.

The Indian caste system (which Karl Marx had characterized

as a negatively analogous development to European feudalism) described the structure and the function of Indian society so long as class relations beyond what is contained by the caste system did not make inroads into it and begin to supplant it. Until then, as an intra-systemic concern, the caste unities changed their relative positions in society from the time the caste system was established in India. Therefore, the formal explanation of 'social change in modern India' as given by M.N. Srinivas (1966), by noting the processes of Sanskritization and Westernization, is not dissimilar to the earlier explanations of 'Aryanization' (as given by A. Lyall in 1882) and 'Brahmanization' (as given by H.H. Risley in 1891).

Later, however, Srinivas attempted a causal explantion of changes in modern India by positing the concept of 'dominant caste', which tends to negate the role of the caste system and relates it to an inter-systemic situation. He describes a 'dominant caste' by the following attributes (1966): (*i*) 'it should own a sizeable amount of the arable land locally available', (*ii*) 'have strength in numbers', (*iii*) 'occupy a high place in the local hierarchy', (*iv*) possess Western education, (*v*) have 'jobs in the administration', and (*vi*) possess 'urban sources of income'. Now, defined in this manner, the dominant caste does not display the characteristics of the caste system in India and only upholds the identification of a caste unity.

On the contrary, caste unity can hardly be discerned precisely by the possession of all six properties: one or some of these properties may be lacking from the identification of a dominant caste. Therefore, the recent sociological (and anthropological) literature in India is replete with imprecise, subjective and contradictory explanations of the so-called dominant caste. However, without going into the loose formulation of the concept, it is obvious that the 'dominant caste' portends the class relations established in Indian society from the British days, namely:

(*i*) property ownership in land, the means of production of the agrarian economy, by any caste—including
the Shudras and the untouchables; (*ii*) demographic viability of a caste, and not according to its order of sacredness;
(*iii*) high position in such a local hierarchy which is not a
replica of the caste structure of society; (*iv*) acquisition of
Western education, which has nothing to do with the
caste system; (*v*) possession of jobs in an administration
which is neither juridically nor culturally caste-based;
and (*vi*) urban sources of income which are beyond the
caste-wise livelihood.

While Srinivas thus postulated a causal explanation of
the systemic changes taking place in modern India by
means of the facade of caste identities, I.P. Desai (1984)
was of the view that caste is not the criterion to appreciate
the mechanics of contemporary Indian society. The 'why'
question of changes in modern India is explained by him
in terms of the social groups which have emerged and are
emerging from the capitalist relations of production and
property. In this context, he would consider the caste
unities to provide a false perception of reality because they
operate, at best, as a 'fossilized class' from a previous systemic order—the Indian variety of feudalism.

G. Omvedt (1978) has moved a step farther from I.P.
Desai while staying further away from Srinivas. She posits
the viewpoint that the poor and the deprived in society
(who also belong to the low castes in the main) are so
oppressed by the rich (who generally belong to the upper
castes) that caste consciousness is revived in a society
where the power in place does not ameliorate their miser-
able existence. Therefore, one may coin an analogy from
Karl Marx's formulation of 'class in itself' and 'class for
itself' (in order to signify class consciousness in the context
of the historicity of class formations) and explain Omvedt's

explication of the persistence of the caste system in modern India (why is it?) in terms of 'caste for itself' besides 'caste in itself'.

In the foregoing analysis, we have cited three rather contrasting explanations of the structural and functional articulations of Indian society, both with and without the caste system. There are other explanations in the same context, which will not be discussed here. The point to note, instead, is that with respect to any phenomenon there may be many causal explanations. Therefore, sciencing society bears the responsibility of ascertaining the relative efficiency of these explanations for answering the 'why is it' question precisely, unequivocally and comprehensively. This task, however, is beyond the pale of observation and deduction, with which social science in general and sociology in particular is presently concerned.

With reference to the same place-, time- and people-bound configuration of world society, one set of observations will deduce one causal explanation (why is it?) in the light of a specific description (what is it?) of the social product and the formal explanation (how is it?) of the social processes working in and on it. Another set of observations may deduce a second causal explanation, and so on, with a third and more causal explanations. As illustrated earlier, all such descriptions and the formal and causal explanations are valid, relevant, and possibly necessary for understanding society. But, in the sequence of answering the what, how and why questions, which one of the causal explanations (or which combination of these explanations) is the most efficient toward unravelling the immanent social processes? This is the question that we should consider next.

The answer to this question will not only clarify the contemporaneous state of affairs in a society but also provide the clue to the answer to the question 'what will it be' with regard to that society. Later, in the light of the answer to the 'what will it be' question, one may systematically (and not as mere proclamation) ask the question 'what should it be?'.

In this context one should bear in mind that these two questions are not confined to understanding society. The perspective is now extended to appraising society with reference to what is 'desirable' and 'undesirable' in the future. Therefore, we should briefly examine how these two questions (what will it be? and what should it be?) may be brought within the orbit of social science, rather than leaving them to philosophical speculations, and the role of sociology in that context.

Appraising Society

Different explanations of why world society (or any one of its configurations) is what it is and how it operates depend, in the ultimate analysis, on the subjective appraisal of social reality by one or the other scholar. The social world comprises the items of information to depict a society as a product and a process. One may conceive the information space that these items form as infinite; but, in practice, the space is found to be enumerable. Therefore, every scholar selects from the infinite but enumerable information space some items as meaningful to present the social structure to explain the what, how and why of society in some manner.

This way, every scholar makes a *primary valuation* of the value-free information space. The information space is value-free because the items of information do not contain any intrinsic value as being wanted by any one or not, as being desirable or undesirable or irrelevant to any person. To put that meaning subjectively would turn an item of information into *datum*, i.e., as possessing a specific meaning. For instance, Srinivas puts datum to each of the six properties of the 'dominant caste', which, by themselves, are mere items of information.

Proceeding a step further, a high order of the same subjectively ascribed meaning to an item of information would turn the subjective datum into an objective datum. We may recall that this is how the 'dominant caste' has become an objective phenomenon in contemporary Indian sociological literature. We may also cite a more common example: perhaps one among a million persons would perceive the colour red as green, and vice versa; and yet, red as red and green as green are objectively treated as data for traffic signals.

Bearing the above analogies in mind, we find that every scholar ascribes a datum to one or the other item of information and, on that basis, structures the yielded data. A structure consists of a mass of information items which are first selected and then articulated in a specific manner with reference to the primary valuation of the social world. Thus, with respect to all available and possible scholars (or, for that matter, all articulate persons), an infinite but enumerable data space is created out of the infinite but enumerable information space. It follows that the efficiency of causal explanations of society depends on how best a particular data structure is created out of all that is possible in order to answer the what, how and why questions regarding a society.

For this purpose it is necessary to distinguish clearly between the structure (which depicts the society as a product) and the process (which denotes changes in the social product). It is also necessary to delineate the relationship between the structure and the process. Let us briefly examine the intricacies of this distinction and interrelation.

Since the social world cannot but be viewed subjectively by a scholar (or anyone, for that matter), his/her perception *deduces*, at first, the structure. The structure may appear to be a matter of *observation*, but one cannot collate all that is observable from the information space. Instead, as noted, a scholar ascribes datum to a specific set of information items and, thus, deduces the social structure.

The scholar, then, *infers* on the social process(es) which has given shape to the depicted structure, and thus answers the question 'why is it'. Very frequently, the scholar proceeds further by envisaging the process(es) acting presently on the structure and, on that basis, provides an answer to the question 'what will it be'. This means that the subjective perception of structure–process– structure (with an inference on the process[es] preceding the initial structure) is an inevitable constraint in viewing society in a state of dynamic equilibrium.

But, then, we are confronted with many formulations of the structure–process–structure (SPS) syndrome for the appraisal of social reality. This is true not only to explain the causality of the present state of society but also to diagnose what the society will be in the near future. The point, therefore, is to ascertain that formulation of the SPS syndrome (or a particular combination of some of the available formulations) which reflects reality in the most precise, unequivocal and comprehensive manner. This point, however, is not always well taken on several grounds.

First, there are those scholars who claim to understand and appraise society in a value-free manner. They declare that their precise and unequivocal observation of what society is and how it operates does not require any preconceived valuation. They also claim that their comprehensive explanation of causality of the initial structure and diagnosis of the anticipated structure refer to those processes which would strike one as a matter of fact. They, thus, take empiricism to an unreal limit because, as noted, valuation is embedded in constructing the data space from the information space.

However, value-free scholars are few because, in present times, the accumulation of knowledge on society as a product and a process is clearly reflected in variable (and often divergent) answers to the what, how, why, and what will be questions raised with respect to the same configuration of world society or human society as a whole. This condition, i.e., the growth of social science knowledge, has given rise to value-accepted scholars.

The value acceptors claim that their description of the what and how of society, their explanation of causality, and their diagnosis of future society have an underpinning of one or the other philosophy and the strategic interpretation of that philosophy as expounded in various theories of a complementary or contradictory nature. Further, at the time of its application, the same theory may be explicated by the scholars in different ways and the data space may accordingly be explored differently. For example, we find today several neoclassical and Marxian theories and their applications to the development of a nation-state. Nonetheless, theory as against gross empiricism is the cue to appraising society from this perspective.

In reality, empiricism and theory are inseparable cues to the appraisal of society in the light of evaluating which formulation of the SPS syndrome is the most precise, unequivocal and comprehensive at the existing state of knowledge in social science. After all, a theory is a past consolidation of empirical knowledge which is considered applicable to the present: it is not a matter of cerebration in vacuum. However, by adhering to one or the other theory, the value acceptors indulge in polemics which generate more heat than shed light on the immanent reality.

As a result, the value acceptors ultimately leave the

appraisal of society to time, but time does not operate in an insular condition. Various viewpoints shaped by theory and empirical knowledge act upon it and define its course. Therefore, unless social science eschews its ordained responsibility, it has a vital role to play in appraising society in the future perspective and monitoring it. The precondition to that role is an evaluation of the relative efficiency of the currently posed SPS syndrome.

This means that a methodology should be devised for a systematic evaluation of the relative efficiency of the formulated SPS syndrome. The nature of the task indicates that the method must be inductive and inferential rather than deductive and positivistic as the individual SPS syndromes are. It will conceive of a value space which accommodates all available and possible SPS syndromes in a *systemically* related manner, i.e., as mutually distinct but interrelated components of a complex whole—the society. On this basis, the methodology should devise means to infer, probabilistically, that SPS syndrome (or a particular combination of several SPS syndromes) which reflects reality the most precisely, unequivocally and comprehensively.

Obviously, this methodology will be based on statistical logic and its accompanying principles and tools. This introductory volume is not suitable for a discussion of this topic. Nonetheless, it should be pointed out that any evaluation of the relative efficiency of the SPS syndromes would require a yardstick which cannot but be the value of life. This point will be briefly examined at the end of this volume.

Value of Life

Scholars and the common people alike have the same outlook to life. They want humans to survive, have security in life, aspire for material prosperity in order to ensure survival and security and lead a wholesome life, and strive for mental progress in order to unfold the potentialities of each human. These four are cardinal valuations for humankind, with which the idealist philosophers are no less concerned than the materialist philosophers.

For example, Shankara preached that the world and this human life are illusion (*maya*), but to preach this doctrine he built monasteries at four corners of his society (which was Bharat in his times) and thus became concerned with the issues of the survival, security, material prosperity and mental progress of his disciples and devotees. This is clearly noticeable today from the role of the Shankaracharyas of these four monasteries.

To consider another example, Yagnavalkya declared that the supreme being is the truth (*iti*) and all manifestations of the world are 'neither this nor that' (*neti neti*). However, he had amassed so much wealth while preaching this unworldly outlook that in his old age he wished to divide his property between two wives. Similar examples of the universal validity of the four cardinal values for human existence may be cited with reference to other idealist philosophers from India and elsewhere.

Survival, security, prosperity and progress are thus the four cardinal values which are encountered by every human in all places, at all times, and with respect to every group of people. Therefore, explicitly or implicitly, humans accept the cardinal valuation of humankind as the yardstick to judge which formulation of the SPS syndrome by the scholars is the most congenial for meeting the value of life, in the context of which society has been created as a product and operates as a process. But there is a catch in employing the yardstick.

The individuals translate the cardinal valuation of life

into different ordinal valuations in accordance with their subjective appreciation of life. Following this, they wish to mould society and operate it according to their respective ordinal valuations. As a result, the cardinal valuation of humankind as the yardstick for evaluating the relative efficiency of the SPS syndromes tends to forfeit its operative meaning.

We should, therefore, find a means to establish on a probability basis that ordinal valuation of the SPS syndrome (or a combination of several syndromes) which is the most akin to the realization of the cardinal valuation of humankind. In this context we find that out of the first stage of demarcation of the ordinal valuations, there are two sets of value of life: one, from the side of the scholars; the other, from the side of the masses.

The scholars, with their consolidated learning, belong to the stratum of elite in society. They define the *needs* of the people for attaining the cardinal values. In that respect, they produce complementary or contradictory philosophical treaties and eventually produce homologous or analogous theories on society as a product and a process. Deductive sociology is entirely concerned with these theories while gross empiricism of the 'value-free' scholars conceals theories because, without *a priori* theoretical orientation, they would have failed to construct the data space from the information space.

The people also appear to be value-free and as concerned with the empirical reality alone. But the manner in which they appreciate reality is value-loaded. This valuation (with the preconceived theorization) emerges from their culture which has been aptly defined by E.B. Tylor (1898) as: 'that complex whole which includes knowledge, belief, art, morals, law, custom, and any other capabilities and habits acquired by man as a member of society.'

Now, in a place-, time- and people-bound configuration

of world society or for human society as a whole, the most dominant ordinal valuation of the elite may synchronize with the most dominant ordinal valuation of the masses. Such a populist situation is seldom noted in history, although some historians tend to oversimplify or conceal contradictions in society. In any case, it is contemporarily non-existent. However, if it occurs at all, social science in general and sociology in particular would enter into a second-order exploration of the value space in order to monitor the extent to which populism meets the quest of humans toward the realization of the cardinal values.

In the circumstances, polemics would be unavoidable and, in fact, necessary. But, as experience tells us, that situation may not arise because nothing moves on a frictionless surface and, therefore, society operates by the resolution of contrary ordinal valuations of life.

What, on the other hand, we are commonly confronted with is that the dominant ordinal valuation of the elite is contrary to the corresponding valuation of the masses. In that event, the elite valuation may be powerfully enforced under dictatorship; but, as history has ordained, that state of affairs is transitory. Similarly, history has shown that a powerful valuation of the masses, contrary to the dominant ordinal valuation of the elite, may lead to civil war in the attempt of humans to realize the cardinal values. Under either of these two circumstances, sociology in the context of social science enters into the ordinal value space constructed by the scholars on the one side, in terms of what the people need, and, on the other, in terms of what the people themselves declare to be what they *want* to have or to get rid of.

These two value spaces require systemic exploration on an inductive base of the social space of the elite and the masses so as to ascertain the points at which the elite's valuation of what the people need is in conjuncture or disjuncture with what the people actually want. This exercise will provide us with an efficient appreciation of what, how and why the immanent social processes are shaping the imminent social structure and what is likely to be (i.e., what will be) the form and content of the social structure in the near future.

Against these systematically and systemically ascertained answers to the above questions, social scientists may evaluate the proximity or distance or the conjectured or disjunctured ordinal valuations of the elite and the masses and, thus, answer the 'what should it be' question of the society in view. Polemics may emerge at this state of critical evaluation of the value of life, but it will not be futile or self-destructive because the social scientists will now be prepared to deal with the third phase of the value of life construct, after having systematically explored the first phase of constructing the data space and the second phase of identifying the value space of the elite and the masses from the overall social space.

Knowledge can proceed only this far because, in the ultimate analysis, it forms an asymptotic relation with reality. It may very closely explicate reality, but never fully and finally. Therefore, science can evermore reduce the gap between the ordinal valuations and the cardinal valuation of humankind, but can never reduce the gap to zero. Any attempt in that respect would lead to what is called *nirvana* in Buddhist beatitude, despite variable interpretations of that concept by different schools of Buddhism. At the state of *nirvana*, subjectivism disappears because Ego (or the person) forfeits its identity, objectivism becomes redundant to the accumulation of knowledge by Ego, and, correspondingly, empiricism forfeits its role in scientific investigation.

The point, therefore, is not to accept the confounding of subjectivism of researchers with the objective reality, which is inevitable in the case of deductive and positivistic orientation to the understanding and appraisal of society. The point is to ascertain, on an inductive and inferential base and on the basis of probability, the *state of objectivity* from the *null* point of subjectivity of the researchers and the researchee alike. This is a matter which cannot be discussed in this introductory volume. It may be pointed out, however, that the procedure would be to search for *commonality* and *discord* in the researchers' and the researchees' perceptions of reality at the existing state of knowledge on society and the universe.

Operationally this would mean that unavoidable imminent appraisals of reality by following the subjectively perceptible structure–process–structure syndrome should be reversed for the appreciation of the immanent process–structure–process syndrome. The shift will facilitate drawing inductive and objective inferences on the state of objectivity from subjectivity, while the inference drawn on a probability basis will be more and more precise along with the continual accumulation of knowledge on reality.

Therefore, all available and empirically ascertainable valuations of life should be conceived to emerge freely from a theoretically infinite but enumerable value space for the appraisal of social reality. It is in this context of postulating the *total* information space, constructing *variable* data spaces, and exploring the *two* value spaces of the elite and the masses that sociology plays a basic and a generic role in the realm of social science for the understanding and the appraisal of society, as briefly discussed in this volume.

CONCLUDING REMARKS

We should bear in mind that appraising society is not the same as understanding society. From understanding society, the course of appraisal extends the horizon of describing the characteristics of a configuration of human society and providing a *formal* explanation of how that society operates with reference to these characteristics. Understanding society has been discussed in Chapter 1. Appraising society brings in, first, the question of a *functional* explanation of why the society operates in a particular manner and not in another. Second, it asks the question of whether in the immediate perspective the society will continue to operate in its contemporaneous manner—what will be of society.

Viewed in this manner, as concluded in Chapter 2, social research takes a turn which has not been, and still is not, commonly undertaken. The turn follows from the five sequential questions which are to be answered by sociology as a generic concern in the realm of social science, which has been the subject matter of Chapter 2. As mentioned earlier, these questions with respect to any phenomenon (society included) are: What is it? How is it? Why is it? What will it be? What should it be? In the context of the last three questions, the previous and the prevailing modes of research in sociology (and anthropology) become, respectively, antiquated and inadequate, and new modes of research become indispensably necessary. We may begin the discussion with reference to the first four of the five questions.

So long as very little or nothing was known about a configuration of human society, the concern of social research was to describe what it is and provide a formal explanation of how it operates as a systemic whole of the integrated parts. In this case the society is assumed to be a constant in its existence and operation. The assumption is no longer justified with the accumulation of knowledge on world society. Therefore, the descriptive mode of research is antiquated and, in view of the dynamic equilibrium of society at any point in time, the formal explanatory mode of research is inadequate because there should be a systematic search for systemic changes in society.

Yet, anchored to the concept of *relative* (and not dynamic equilibrium), anthropological and sociological research (in India, in particular) is usually confined to the descriptive or the formally explanatory mode by treating the society in view as *systemically constant*—as if the changes take place within a society as relative to other societies, but all these societies are treated as belonging to one constant system. The horizon is not extended by treating the society as *systemically variable* and appraising it on that account. An analogy may help to understand the two different perspectives.

We may state that the sun rises in the east and sets in the west. We may also ascertain how it thus behaves constantly with reference to any place and time for the world societies. An explanation is involved in answering the question 'how is it' in this manner (namely, the reason for the sun always rising in the east and setting in the west), but this explanation follows automatically from the answer to the 'how' question regarding the sun and the earth. But, if we wish to understand at which point on the eastern horizon, as viewed from a particular place and at a specific time, the sun as an object rises and, correspondingly, sets on the western horizon, we become involved with a *system of variation* in its place, time and object dimensions: the behaviour of the sun, then, is no longer constant.

Accordingly, the question, 'why does the position of the sun in the eastern and the western horizons vary by place and time?' acquires a meaning of its own. It is not submerged in the question, 'how does the sun vary from point to point in the eastern and the western horizons?', which retains its distinctive relevance to characterize the system of variation. Next, therefore, we ask the question, 'what will it be', with reference to the probabilistic position of the sun in the eastern and the western horizons as viewed for the future from different place and time coordinates of the earth.

Thus, when we have answered the set of four questions—

what, how, why and *what will be*—with respect to an *objective* phenomenon (i.e., a phenomenon which is not concerned with variations from person to person, or Ego, in their subjective perceptions), our appreciation of its particular system of variation is complete. We have not only learnt of its characteristics and operation but also of its causality and predictive behaviour in the time to come.

With reference to a phenomenon or a set of phenomena, we may conceptualize the systems of variation in an increasingly exhaustive and complicated manner in order to appreciate reality evermore precisely and comprehensively. The process will evidently call for more and more exhaustive and complicated answers to the four questions we have posed. However, they would be applicable unequivocally to the appraisal of any system of variation because the first question (what is it?) refers to the description of the system, the second (how is it?) to its classification (i.e., an analysis of its internal articulations and variations as well as its interrelationships with other systems), the third (why is it?) to an explanation or its causality, and the fourth (what will it be?) to the predictability of the structure, function and process of the system of variation in the future.

As individual researchers, we may deal with one, some, or all of the four questions, or give them unequal emphasis when dealing with more than one question, according to our resources, inclination and ability. But, as a community of scientists, we should deal with all of them, and with equal emphasis, in order that we may accumulate knowledge on the phenomenon in a precise and objective manner by means of the system of variation examined. However, in social research, a wide variation is noticeable in this respect both conceptually and operationally.

There was a time in empirical social research when we laid particular stress on the first question, dealt in passing

with the second, rather ignored the third, and did not consider the fourth within our terms of reference. On the
other hand, non-empirical social research used to be engrossed with speculation and conjecture on the third and
the fourth questions, with little adulteration from answers
to the first two. Seldom was an attempt made to draw a
sequential, objective and logically consistent link among
all the four questions with reference to a circumscribed or
a universal topic.

Today, empirical social research tends to pay serious
attention to the first three questions of *what*, *how* and *why*,
but the answer to the third is either a matter of almost
automatic deduction from that to the second or a reference
to a theory. Seldom is there an attempt to answer the three
questions through an analysis of their respective characteristics from the grass-roots level. Further, the fourth
question is almost always avoided as 'unscientific', although
with respect to the live phenomena in a society we may
not be averse to *implying* 'what will it be' in the light of our
answers to the first three questions.

The relative importance of the four questions becomes
clear when we specify the purpose of social research. If
our objective is to do a piece of 'natural history', obviously
the emphasis will be on description and classification of a
phenomenon. This will involve an analysis of its characteristics and subsequently an analysis of its interrelations
with the associated phenomena. In this context, the third
question is virtually irrelevant; the fourth is out of the pic-
ture.

On the other hand, if we define the purpose of social research as to explain a system of variation, the first three
questions attain equal relevance, but we may get away
with the allocation of a secondary position to the third
question because, in spite of our casual treatment of the
why **question and neglect of the 'what will it be' question,**

we may be able to explain the role of a system of variation in a historically accomplished situation as it is then, place- and time-bound at both ends. Consequently, within the place-time limits, the answer to the first two questions, 'what is it' and 'how is it', can more or less explain the dynamics of the system in the sense of suggesting plausible reasons for the *end* result.

However, with this coverage of information we cannot proceed to *diagnose* the probabilistic role of a system of variation for the future because we are then faced with the condition that its place-time terminals are free at one end—the contemporary perspective. This is obvious for the time dimension, and the place dimension also must be free because no one knows for certain the spatial extension of the system in the future. For example, nation-building in the subcontinent of India enlarged its form and content from being only 'Indian' up to 1947, with East Bengal forming a part of the newly emerged system, Pakistan. But, since 1971, it has assumed a new form and content with the formation of Bangladesh.

Thus, a system of variation may assume one of several possible roles, and the prediction of the *most probable* role may be left either to our imagination or to an appraisal of 'what is it', 'how is it', and 'why is it' of the system from the grass-roots level. It is only by the second procedure that we learn about the viability, propensity and proliferation of a system of variation with respect to different stimuli. This will denote the *specific conditions* and the *degree of probability* under which the system may assume a particular structure, function in a particular manner, and undergo a suggested process of change or register casual fluctuations around a central tendency.

These comments are not meant to deride the excellence of many descriptive and explanatory studies. It is also not our contention to undermine the necessity of producing theories or making use of the available ones, which was once decried by gross empiricism and its echo is not yet completely lost. But we ought to bear in mind that while a theory answers the 'why is it' and 'how is it' questions, it must be place-, time-, and object-specific. The efficiency of a theory is, therefore, appraised by the extension of its place, time and object limits.

A theory should ultimately surpass these limitations, but it can never do so fully and finally as it would then foreclose the quest for knowledge. Therefore, our comments follow from continual efforts to improve the course of social research without undermining what has been achieved so far. In that context, our task is to clarify the role that theory is to play with reference to the objective of our study.

There are two ways in which a theory may be used in social research. It may be used as a *yardstick* to explain a phenomenon or a system or variation on a *deductive* basis. Alternatively, a theory may be used in the form of (or in the course of formulating) an 'alternate hypothesis'. In the second instance, its efficiency is to be tested on an *inductive* base in order to appraise its *relative* efficiency vis-à-vis other such hypotheses formulated for understanding the aspect of reality under consideration.

For the first procedure, a theory is employed as a model to give an appropriate fit to the variations noticed in the 'what is it' and 'how is it' of a system of variation, and thus utilize it to answer the question, 'why is it'. The use of theory in this manner is *valid* when we examine a system of variation in a place- and time-bound situation. But a second researcher may employ another theory claiming to obtain a 'better fit' with the available data and, thus, turn both the theories into 'alternate hypotheses'.

In this context, the point is not only of the validity of a theory but also of its efficiency. This distinction leads us towards diagnostic research (and not mere explanatory research) with reference to a closed circuit in place and time, as we shall examine later. For the present we should note that both the validity and efficiency of using a theory as a yardstick would be lost when we examine a system of variation in the contemporary perspective and with the crucial objective of answering the question, 'what will it be'. In that context, the second use of theory comes directly into effect. Obviously, if a theory could automatically denote 'what will it be', there would have been no need for further research.

This means that the plausible theories should represent one aspect of our *a priori* knowledge, the other aspect being given by the empirical findings with respect to 'what is it', how is it', and 'why is it', This is no less true for a place- and time-bound situation than for a place- and time-open situation. As noted, the above-mentioned two researchers concerned with a place- and time-bound situation employ theories as different yardsticks but, in fact, treat them as 'alternate hypotheses'. Thus, with reference to a closed or open circuit of place, time and people dimensions of reality, the theories attain the status of hypotheses to be tested, although they have been tested previously with respect to the place, the time, and the people dimensions of variation they comprehend and however extensively and intensively they might have been found to take note of these variations in the past.

Therefore, we may agree that if the objective of research is purely descriptive and classificatory, as in 'natural history', any theory is hardly of relevance and the strategy of research is 'fact finding' and the interpretation of the 'facts' with reference to the two questions 'what is it' and 'how is it' (i.e., the description and formal operation of the phenomenon). If the objective of research is explanatory in a place- and time-bound situation, a theory may be used as

a yardstick in a *deductive-positivistic* manner in order to answer the third question, 'why is it'; but the answer may not
be unequivocal. Therefore, if the objective of research is
diagnostic in a place- and time-open or closed situation,
the plausible theories should be used as hypotheses to be
tested on an *inductive-inferential* base so as to determine
their relative efficiency for the appraisal of social reality.
All the four questions, 'what is it', 'how is it', 'why is it',
and 'what will it be' would be answered on that basis.

Thus, by considering theory and practice together, we
may make the following points regarding an effective pursuit of social research:

1. With reference to a system of variation which may
refer to one or more phenomena (in whichever manner a
phenomenon or a system of variation may be identified so
long as it maintains logical consistency and distinctiveness), descriptive research answers the questions 'what is
it' and 'how is it', explanatory research answers additionally the question 'why is it' in a restricted manner, and
diagnostic research answers all the three questions and,
furthermore, the question 'what will it be'.

2. Speculation on 'why is it' and conjecture on 'what will
it be' from descriptive research, or on 'what will it be' from
explanatory research, are not unknown. So long as such
speculation and conjecture are kept separate from research
findings, no harm is done as they would be considered at
their face value. But concerted attempts made to answer
these questions from descriptive and explanatory research
yield inefficient results. The attempts may also be harmful
because the three approaches to social research have different orders of potentiality for the appraisal of a system of
variation.

3. Explanatory research is usually distinguished from
descriptive research as involving a distinct method, i.e., a
different procedure for an orderly arrangement of the

proposals, data, analysis and interpretation of the results of research. But diagnostic research is commonly regarded to be a part of explanatory research and is assumed to follow the same orientation and methodology while being distinguished by certain techniques to be employed with reference to a particular programme. For example, diagnostic research is considered necessary to 'welfare sociology'. For a similar reason, diagnostic research is regarded as an appendage to the 'sociology of development .

4. Therefore, it would be useful to distinguish among the descriptive, explanatory and diagnostic modes of research because any one of them may be favoured by a researcher in accordance with his/her inclination, ability and resources; however, he/she should be aware of the scope and limitation of the respective modes. The researcher may thus make his/her efforts worthwhile within the sphere of knowledge one has elected for onself to be confined within rather than trespassing into others.

5. Because of its terms of reference to elicit answers to only two questions, 'what is it' and 'how is it', with respect to a system of variation, the orientation and methodology of descriptive research would obviously be deductive. The additional term of reference to answer the 'why is it' question does not invariably require a shift in the orientation of explanatory research from the descriptive because (i) the contour and content of the system of variation to be examined are specified by its place-time coordinates, i.e., the limits are imposed, and (ii) the course of research is geared to substantiate a causal explanation in the light of a prevailing theory or a hypothesis evolved out of empirical findings. However, inductive techniques enter into the methodology of explanatory research in order to apply the concept of probability in testing the validity of the theoretical or hypothesized causal explanation.

6. On the other hand, for diagnostic research the future limit of the system of variation under examination cannot be fixed by the place-time coordinates because the *ultimate* term of reference is to answer the question, 'what will it be'. For the 'open' system, therefore, the answer to the 'why is it' question cannot be obtained from an explanatory theory or empirically formulated hypothesis. It is now necessary to ascertain from the grass-roots level the viability, propensity and proliferation of the system of variation in respect of different stimuli so as to predict, on a probability basis, the future course of behaviour of the system.

7. Thus, the question 'why is it' assumes greater significance for diagnostic than for explanatory research. All that is known and *knowable* regarding the system of variation under examination (i.e., from theory and empirical findings) will now have to be marshalled together in order that the relevant theories and *a priori* hypotheses form a systematically ordered series of *alternate hypotheses*. These are to be tested against an appropriate *null* hypothesis, i.e., under the imposed assumption that none of the alternate hypotheses is valid. This strategy is required to find an unequivocal answer to the ultimate question by refuting the *null* hypothesis and thus proving the most stringent validity of one of the alternate hypotheses.

8. It follows that since the most stringent validity of any one of all available and possible alternate hypotheses will always be an open question, the course of diagnostic research will be evermore precise and comprehensive under the assumption that the alternate hypotheses form an *infinite but enumerable* series which emerge *unrestrictedly* from the field of variation dealing with the 'open' system. Evidently, the alternate hypotheses will be successively formulated in a fuller and better form as knowledge on the field of variation under examination accumulates. Therefore, the orientation of diagnostic research must be inductive

and inferential, and its methodology would involve a constant interaction between the deductive and inductive techniques.

9. The inductive-inferential orientation and the corresponding methodology will also be relevant to explanatory research if more than one theory or empirically formulated hypotheses are employed to ascertain which one of them gives the *best possible fit* to answering the 'why is it' question regarding the system of variation under examination. In this case, an explanation of causality in the system may be sought from a predetermined and specified set of theories and *a priori* hypotheses but with the conceptual understanding that more and more theories and *a priori* hypotheses may be brought under examination, as in the case of diagnostic research.

10. Therefore, the deductive-positivistic orientation to research would now be inadequate to answer the 'why is it' question because none of the adopted theories and hypotheses may be employed as a yardstick for explanation. Instead, all these theories and hypotheses would be formulated as alternate hypotheses around an appropriate *null* hypothesis so as to explain which one (or none) of them can best explain the system of variation under examination. But, conducted in this manner, explanatory research would forfeit its *raison d'être* to explain causality in terms of only one theory or hypothesis. Instead, it would turn into diagnostic research *within the circuit of a place- and time-bound situation* and with the 'what will it be' question germane to answering the 'why' question.

11. If we undertake a rigorous course of analysis of a system of variation with reference to the structure, function and processes involved in its internal articulations, variations and interrelationships with other systems (even though the systems may be confined to a place- and time-bound situation), then the relevance of the 'what will it be'

question would be automatically implied in answering the question, 'why is it'. This is illustrated, for example, by an examination of feudalism as a world system and in the course of its variation in European, Asian and other contexts.

12. The point is also notable in the case of a historically-bound discussion on the modern world system or the Indian social system, which will obviously deal with the pre-feudal, feudal and the succeeding stages of social development. Similarly, the 'what will it be' question emerges automatically (with its probabilistic content formulated in an increasingly precise and comprehensive manner) if, even within a historically-bound situation, we examine the 'why' question with reference to various theories and *a priori* hypotheses; for example, in the context of the caste system in India. In this case, the limited possibilities of explanatory research on the basis of one theory employed as a yardstick would be transformed into virtually unlimited possibilities of diagnostic research on the basis of several theories considered simultaneously.

13. Thus, descriptive research has little scope of appraising social reality. Explanatory research on the basis of a theory or hypothesis employed as a yardstick for explanation has more but still limited scope because it may produce an equivocal, imprecise, or incomprehensive answer to the question 'why is it'. The explanation would become more and more unequivocal, precise and comprehensive as more than one theory and *a priori* hypotheses are considered simultaneously for answering the 'why' question in the light of their *relative explanatory power*. But explanatory research is then transformed into diagnostic research even within a place- and time-bound situation.

14. On the other hand, when the place-time coordinates of the system of variation under examination are free in the contemporary perspective and the purpose of research

is to describe, classify, explain and predict 'what will it be' of the system by means of probabilistic inference, diagnostic research becomes the only means to appraise social reality. In this way, the conceptual and the methodological distinctiveness of diagnostic research holds its ground.

15. However, summarized as above, the three modes of research are seen to be liable to a course of systematization while maintaining their mutually distinct character. This point will be clear from Charts 1, 2 and 3.

It can be noted from Chart 3 that by means of a sustained interaction of deductive and inductive techniques on an inductive-inferential base, the diagnostic approach would organize research activities as a systematic and continuous effort toward unfolding social reality. As seen from Chart 2, the explanatory approach would correspondingly be limited in scope, while comments on the descriptive approach are hardly necessary at the current state of social research. However, it may appear that from the manner in which diagnostic research has been conceived and operationalized that it will be effective only when quantified information is available for evolving indicators, testing hypotheses, and so on. Strictly speaking, this is a matter for discussion on the methodological aspect of diagnostic research which is beyond the scope of the present volume. But we may point out here that this is more a matter of mathematical thinking than of quantification in social science.

Discrete series of quantities (e.g., the proportional occurrence of an attribute) can be prepared any time from the qualitative data. Continuous series of quantitative variates are also not infrequent at the present state of social research. Therefore, unless we evolve appropriate methods to deal with the qualitative data and also employ mathematical principles to quantify them properly, the state of social research will not improve beyond its present position.

CHART 1

Mode of Research	Descriptive	Explanatory	Diagnostic
Object' of research	A constant phenomenon or a system of variation	A system of variation	A system of variation
Place-time coordinates of field of observation	Specified at a point or forms a closed circuit	A closed circuit	An open circuit; free at the contemporary terminal
Scope of research	Description, classification	Description, classification, explanation	Description, classification, explanation, prediction
Terms of reference to answer question:	What is it? How is it?	What is it? How is it? Why is it?	What is it? How is it? Why is it? What will it be?
Orientation	Deductive-positivistic	Deductive-positivistic	Inductive-inferential
Role of theory	Implicit in what is described and classified	Yardstick for causal explanation	Produce alternate hypotheses in an infinite but enumerable series for causal explanation and probabilistic prediction
Role of empirical findings	Ascertain internal characteristics and classify vis-à-vis analogous constant phenomena or systems of variation	Characterize, classify and formulate one hypothesis for causal explanation	Characterize, classify and produce alternate hypotheses in the same manner and for the same purpose as regarding theory

CHART 2

Organization of Activities to Answer the Fundamental Questions

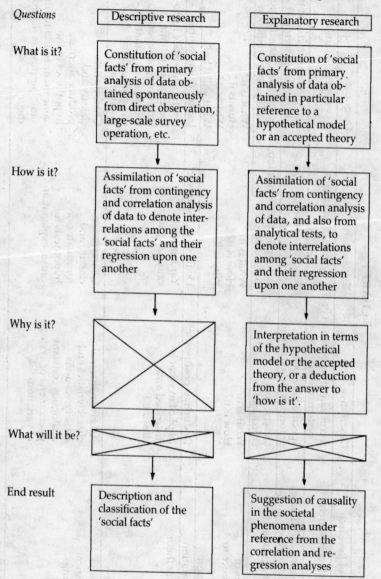

Questions	Descriptive research	Explanatory research
What is it?	Constitution of 'social facts' from primary analysis of data obtained spontaneously from direct observation, large-scale survey operation, etc.	Constitution of 'social facts' from primary analysis of data obtained in particular reference to a hypothetical model or an accepted theory
How is it?	Assimilation of 'social facts' from contingency and correlation analysis of data to denote interrelations among the 'social facts' and their regression upon one another	Assimilation of 'social facts' from contingency and correlation analysis of data, and also from analytical tests, to denote interrelations among 'social facts' and their regression upon one another
Why is it?		Interpretation in terms of the hypothetical model or the accepted theory, or a deduction from the answer to 'how is it'.
What will it be?		
End result	Description and classification of the 'social facts'	Suggestion of causality in the societal phenomena under reference from the correlation and regression analyses

CHART 3

Organization of Activities to Answer the Fundamental Questions
by Diagnostic Research

Stage t   Stage t$_j$

Constitution of 'social facts' from primary analysis of the basic data classified by place, time and object dimensions of the phenomena and systems of variation examined, as obtained by (a) retrieval of the inventorized information, and (b) planned collection of data from the *total* field of variation to fulfil the gaps in the information available

What is it?

Assimilation of 'social facts' from contingency and correlation analysis of data and also from analytical tests to denote interrelations among 'social facts' and their regression upon one another

How is it?

Probabilistic prediction of 'what will it be' from the appraisal of the viability, propensity and proliferation of the phenomena and systems of variation, in the light of the results from the tests of alternate hypotheses

What will it be?

Evaluation of the nature and degree of alignment of the 'social facts', in reference to the problem in view, so as to formulate indicators denoting the positive, negative, or neutral aspects of variation in the phenomena and systems of variation under examination.

Formulation of alternative hypotheses in the light of the 'theoretical' and 'practical' knowledge on the problem in view, and allocation of an order of priority to the hypotheses according to the positive, negative and neutral characteristics of the indicators and their relative importance within each characteristic.

Test of the serially ordered alternate hypotheses, and the appraisal of the results of the tests, in order to ascertain causality in the phenomena and systems of variation.

Why is it?

Today we are faced, on the one hand, with uncritical quantification of social data leading to fallacious formulations, arid abstractions, or superficial (and sometimes wrong) generalizations. On the other hand, we are faced with the viewpoint that social research cannot be based on a mathematical and statistical foundation because of its intrinsic characteristics. But, if quantification means the abstraction and summation of knowledge, there is no reason why it cannot be applied to 'social data'. Of course, the point will always be valid, as in the case of all forms of sciencing, that the course of abstraction and summation of 'social data' must not be divorced from reality. This is not infrequently found in social research from the crusaders of quantification.

However, mathematical thinking is much more than the mere application of some statistical tools for analysis and the interpretation of the results of the analysis in terms of certain 'levels of significance'. Primarily, its job is to systemize (i.e., systematically divide and collect into an integrated and complex whole) our ever-accumulating knowledge. Under this fall the proposals of diagnostic research. Therefore, this course of research will bridge the gap between the language of theory and research: a gap which some scholars have thought to be insurmountable.

However, this task for social research is not completely accomplished by answering the four questions: *what is it? how is it? why is it?* and *what will it be?* That will be true for the objective world which would exist irrespective of a person, a self, the Ego. In that context, 'what will it be' is the terminal question, and the question 'what should it be' is irrelevant because, *in itself*, the objective world is beyond individual preference. On the other hand, with respect to the social world, the last question that emerges is 'what should it be', which is equally true for the objective world *for itself*, i.e., in the context of the social world.

As noted earlier, the 'what should it be' question emerges in the light of the cardinal valuation of humankind, which has four main components: (*i*) survival of the species, (*ii*) security of the people in their lifespan, (*iii*) material prosperity of individuals to ensure survival, security and wholesome living, and (iv) mental progress of each person in order that his/her potentialities can be unfolded. Individuals differ in translating these four components of cardinal valuation into their own ordinal valuations. Therefore, their value preferences raise the 'what should it be' question as the last one in the series of five for the appraisal of social reality.

It is useful to note in this connection that when dealing with the objective world, one is confronted with the 'what should it be' question *after* any one of its manifestations has been understood at the best possible state of existing knowledge. For example, after realizing the potential effects of nuclear fission (i.e., 'what will it be'), the 'what should it be' question emerges to harness this manifestation of the objective world (viz., nuclear energy) for peaceful purposes like the generation of electricity or for making nuclear weapons. It will be noticed that in this context, 'what should it be' is a social question, which is embedded in the case of all manifestations of the social world after answering the questions what, how, and why is it, and what will it be.

This is so because the social world is concerned with individuals (subjects) to begin with, and with the exploration of the congruity of the subjects for the realization of the value of life. Therefore, the individuals in a society do not act for and evaluate life in a random and indiscriminate manner. As discussed in Chapter 1, if they did so, the society would not have been formed. On the contrary, therefore, the subjects act and value life in such a manner that actions and valuations form distinctive patterns—complementary or contradictory.

It follows that the more precisely, unequivocally and comprehensively the patterns are distinguished in the social world, the more the social world attains objectivity, that is, manifestations of a nature which is not subject to casual differences among individuals. It also follows that by the extent of this kind of objectivity from the subjectivity of all individuals, the social world may be explored irrespective of individual wills, i.e., until and unless these wills form new patterns by attaining the group character, are institutionalized, and thus reflected in the social relationship, social behaviour, and social action of the people.

In this way, the prognosis of the question, 'what should it be', enters into social research as beyond diagnosis by answering the question, 'what will it be'. However, as discussed in Chapter 2 in the context of 'value of life', the prognosis is not the prerogative of social philosophers or experts in social science. They do not have the monopoly of translating the cardinal valuation of humankind into ordinal valuations of one or another kind; such as, in the ultimate sense, traversing the social world from mind to matter or from matter to mind.

On the contrary, the task is a coordination of (i) an appraisal of the elite-experts' valuations of what the people *need* in their quest for realizing the cardinal valuation of humankind, (ii) an appraisal of the individually formed groups' valuations of what the people themselves *want* in the same context, and (iii) the conclusions to be drawn from the interactions of these two sets of appraisal of social reality in a place-, time-, and people-specific situation. This point has been noted at the end of Chapter 2. It should be noted further that in this respect social research enters into an almost virgin field which falls within the terms of reference of sociology as a specific and a generic concern in the realm of social science. Therefore, this is a field without the exploration of which systemic sociology would not be able to fully meet its terms and conditions.

REFERENCES

Callard, K. 1957. *Pakistan: A Political Study*. London, George Allen & Unwin.

Desai, I.P. 1984. 'Should "Caste" be the Basis for Recognizing Backwardness?', *Economic and Political Weekly*, 19(28): 1106–16.

Engels, F. 1951. *Karl Marx and Frederick Engels: Selected Works in Two Volumes*. Moscow, Foreign Languages Publishing House.

Fisher, R.A. 1946, *Statistical Methods for Research Workers*. London, Oliver and Boyd.

Khan, A.M. 1960. 'Research about Muslim Aristocracy in East Pakistan', in P. Bessaignet (ed.), *Social Research in East Pakistan*, pp.17–29. Dacca, Asiatic Society of Pakistan.

Lyall, A. 1882. *Asiatic Studies*. London, John Murray.

Marx, K. 1942. *The German Ideology*. London, Lawrence & Wishart.

———— 1951. *Karl Marx and Frederick Engels: Selected Works in Two Volumes*. Moscow, Foreign Languages Publishing House.

Morgan, L.H. 1964. *Ancient Society*. Cambridge, Massachusetts, The Belknap Press of Harvard University Press (first edition, New York).

Mukerjee, R.K. 1961. 'A Philosophy of Social Science', Presidential Address to the Third All-India Sociological Conference, 1958, in R.N. Saksena (ed.), *Sociology, Social Research and Social Problems in India*, pp.46–52. Bombay, Asia Publishing House.

Mukerji, D.P. 1958. 'Indian Tradition and Social Change', in *Diversities: Essays in Economics, Sociology and other Social Problems*. New Delhi, People's Publishing House (Presidential Address to the First All-India Sociological Conference, 1955).

Omvedt, G. 1978. 'Class Struggle or Caste War', *Frontier*, 11.

Risley, H.H. 1891. *The Tribes and Castes of Bengal*, 2 vols. Calcutta, Bengal Secretariat Press.

Robbins, L. 1932. *The Nature and Significance of Economic Science*. London, Macmillan.

Sayeed, K.B. 1967. *The Political System of Pakistan*. Boston, Houghton Miffin Co.

Srinivas, M.N. 1966. *Social Change in Modern India*. Bombay, Allied Publishers.

Sweezy, P.M. 1946. *The Theory of Capitalist Development*. London, Dennic Dobson.

Tylor, E.B. 1898. *Primitive Culture*, vol. I. London, John Murray.

Weber, M. 1947. *The Theory of Social and Economic Organization*. London, William Hodge & Co.